RING THE CHIEF JUSTICE

The quirky adventures of an Australian journalist in Africa

JOHN LAWRENCE

ARCADIA

Published in 2020 by ARCADIA
a literary imprint of Australian Scholarly Publishing Pty Ltd
7 Lt Lothian St Nth, North Melbourne, Victoria 3051
tel 03 9329 6963 / fax 03 9329 5452
enquiry@scholarly.info / www.scholarly.info

First published in Australia 2020
This edition published 2020

Cover design, typesetting: WorkingType (www.workingtype.com.au)

Featured on the cover: Chief Atanda Fatai Williams, Chief Justice of Nigeria; Former Kenyan President Daniel Arap Moi; and the assassinated Nigerian head of state, General Murtala Muhammed.

ISBN: 978-1-9259848-1-1

For Diana (Dinny), my partner-in-crime,
and to the memory of the late John Lahey.

About the author

Melbourne-born John Lawrence is a veteran journalist, having held senior positions in Australia, China and East and West Africa. This book, his first, traces his adventures in Nigeria and Kenya, his face-to-face encounter with a gunman and his deportation from Kenya where his column *The Cutting Edge* exposed graft and corruption. He lives in Carlton North, Victoria, with his wife, Diana, and two miniature Dachshunds.

Author's note

My wife, Diana Lawrence, will be known by many readers as Dinny, her family nickname. Be assured they are one and the same person.

Foreword

Time spent in Africa stays in the heart and the memory. Old Africa hands will find much to remember and enjoy in these pages. Back in the closing years of British Colonial Africa there always seemed to be jobs for expatriate journalists in places like Kenya, Uganda, and Northern Rhodesia (now Zambia). Most of the reporters and sub editors who filled them were from the United Kingdom and there were a few from Australia and New Zealand.

Independence pretty much put an end to that era but it created opportunities for a different breed of expatriate journalist, the *Training Editor.* John Lawrence was one of the most experienced (and peripatetic) of these and his work took him around the world, from Mauritius to China, from Africa to the Caribbean. We have been colleagues and friends for more than 50 years but Australia is the only country in which we have both worked at the same time.

This charming and evocative memoir recalls his Africa years, Nigeria (1977–1979) and Kenya (1986–1994), accompanied by his wife Diana and their daughter Imogen. Eleven years of seminars and training punctuated by adventures in game parks and on the East African coast, a near death experience with a hippopotamus, robbed at gunpoint in a Nairobi leather goods shop.

John Lawrence has a well developed sense of the absurd and his memoir is peppered with humorous insights and asides. Among the best of them is this advice to a pregnant Diana from her medical specialist in Lagos: 'In an emergency ring the Chief Justice. He has a phone and it works.'

John Tidey

Melbourne, 2020

Contents

Introduction

Go into the street, any street, and conduct this experiment: strike up a conversation with passersby and pose the question: "What do you know about Africa?" The answer, more than likely, will be something like this: "I don't know much about that country, but I would like to go there some time to see the wild animals."

And therein lies the rub. Most people see Africa as a country and not a continent. Africa, in fact, is 54 countries. It is a huge continent of 1.111 billion people speaking some 2000 languages. It is spread over 30.2 million square kilometres or one-fifth of the world's land surface. Only Asia is bigger.

Compare this with the smallest continent on Earth — Australia. Just one country and only 25 million people to occupy its 7.69 million square kilometres. Its inhabitants — the first nation people — speak 150 languages.

There are, of course, physical similarities. Both Africa and Australia have tropical and temperate regions, and both have big deserts in the middle. In Africa, however, the Sahara continues to march south at an alarming rate.

Africa is the continent that promised so much, but was never allowed to fulfil that promise. For centuries European nations eyed the "Dark Continent". As early as the 15th century the Portuguese were the first European power to tap into the riches of Nigeria on the west coast."Lagos", the former capital, for example, is Portuguese for "Lake", and its legacy can be seen in the design of some of the old buildings.

In more recent times, large chunks of east, west and southern Africa were colonised by the German powerhouse: Burundi, Cameroon, Namibia, Tanganyika (now Tanzania) and Togo. The Germans also controlled large parts of Chad, Gabon, Ghana, Kenya, Mozambique, Nigeria, Central African Republic and the Congo.

At the infamous Berlin conference of 1884–85, fourteen European countries met to divide the spoils. Countries that gained the most were France, Germany, Great Britain and Portugal. After the Allied forces invaded the German-controlled Territories in 1919, the League of Nations, the pre-cursor to the UN, divided them between Belgium, France, Portugal, South Africa and Britain.

Independence began in 1957 when the West African country of Ghana was granted its freedom. And then came the great freedom push, partly galvanised by Harold Macmillan in his famous speech to the South African parliament on 3 February 1960:

"The wind of change is blowing through this continent. Whether we like it or not, this growth of national consciousness is a political fact."

This was the era when colonial powers collapsed like dominos. Thirty-two countries alone became independent in the 1960s. Before this, Britain and France were each the colonial master of

A relief map of the vast African continent.

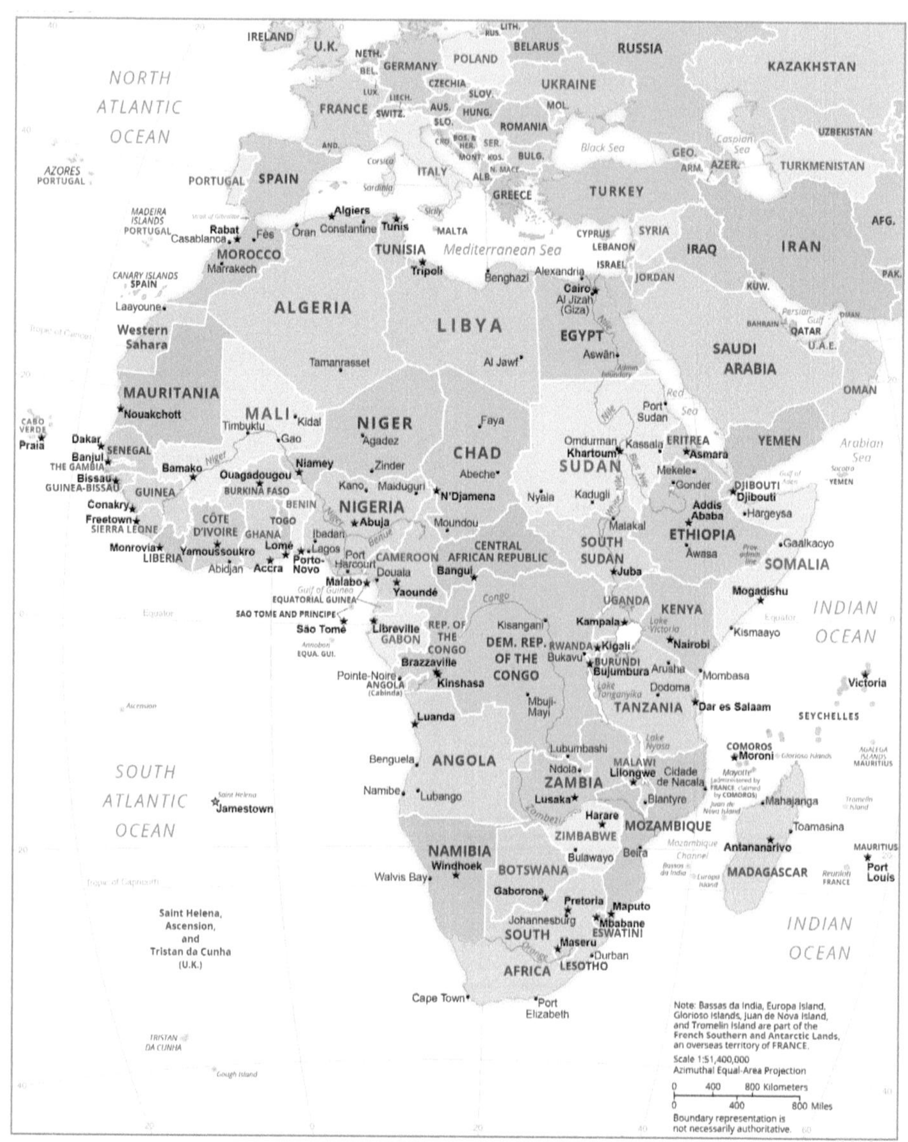

The 54 African states.

20 African countries a staggering 40 out of 53 (South Sudan, the 54th, gained independence in 2011).

Britain annexed Lagos in 1861 and by 1906 controlled all of Nigeria until it gained independence in 1960. Kenya gained *Uhuru* (Independence) in 1963.

However, this memoir is neither a history lesson, nor a political dissertation. References to political upheavals and ethnic violence are generally used only when they are essential to the narrative. This then is a book about the experiences of Diana and myself, the people we met, the wonderful game and the spellbinding scenery.

Today both Nigeria, the most populous black nation on earth with 190.8 million people and Kenya (Pop. 49.6 million) are at a crossroads. They face enormous challenges and an uncertain future.

However, as the late Derek Ingram, co-founder of the Commonwealth Journalists Association and a lifelong champion of developing nations, once told me: The history to date of Africa is but the blink of an eyelid.

Part One

Chapter 1

SAY YOUR PRAYERS

It was a sunny Saturday morning in busy Moktar Daddah Street on the edge of Nairobi's CBD. In the leather goods shop, my friend Batuk Jethwa and his staff were winding down for the weekend. Just myself and a handful of customers remained.

In one corner, a tall smiling African man was rummaging through a large bag of remainder sandals and flip flops. The tall man dived into the bag and came up with a pair of flip-flops.

"How much for these?" he asked the counter staff.

That was as far as he got as the peace of the day was shattered.

Bang!

A bolt on the heavy front door was slammed shut.

Bang!

The second bolt was rammed home.

For a split second there was deathly quiet. And then an order was barked:

"Don't move. This is a hold-up."

The "customers" had guns in their hands. We were being robbed.

At the same time the tall African, who had been standing next to me, spun around from the flip fop bag and pointed a pistol at my head.

"Quick. Get down," he ordered. He was a polite bandit. He actually added "Please". Confronted by a six foot, four inch man with a gun, you do as you are told. I hit the deck and lay face-down on the floor. The tall man looked down and I could he see rather fancied my wrist watch.

"Give me your watch," he said. I gave him my watch.

"Now, your money. Give me your money."

"I don't have much money, only a few shillings." (The local currency.)

"Give it to me" he repeated. His voice was impatient. Urgent. I had tight jeans on. It's rather hard to filch notes from the front pocket when you are face-down on a hard floor. With difficulty I managed to get the money out.

At the same time, the tall Kenyan's accomplices were robbing everyone, genuine customers and staff alike, of their possessions. But the big prize was the accumulated takings.

One of the bandits turned on Batuk: "Now where have you hidden the real money," he shouted. There was menace in his voice and body language.

Batuk pointed to the cash register.

"Over there," he said.

The bandits emptied the till. The pickings were poor: A few notes, loose change. Cheques.

Batuk was not the sort to panic. Coolly he said: "My friend there are only receipts and cheques in there. No cash."

"Eh bwana, you no go mess with me. On your knees. Say your prayers. I count to 10. You bring me the money or I shoot you."

It was like talk from a gangster movie and would have been comical without the deadly intent. Batuk didn't hesitate. With his life on the line he blurted out: "Okay, okay, I'll get it for you" and produced the hidden money.

The tall Kenyan bandit had not forgotten me. But he seemed at a loss to know what to do with me. After an awkward pause, he had solved the problem.

"Right. Out the back," he ordered and escorted me to a back room toilet.

"Now get inside. I'll lock you in."

"But there's no lock on the outside."

"Then you lock yourself in from the inside," he said helpfully.

High drama had turned to farce. I locked myself in and waited. After two or three minutes, everything went quiet. I heard myself call out in a strangled little voice.

"Is it all right to come out now?"

The gangsters had gone.

I ran to the front doors, now wide open, and out into the street to see my car double-parked. But where was Diana, who had come to pick me up? Suddenly a head popped up from under the dashboard where she had ducked as two uniformed policemen strolled by.

"I thought I might get a ticket," she said.

"We have all just been robbed at gunpoint," I yelled. "Where are those policemen?"

"If you hurry, you might just catch them before they turn the corner."

I sprinted down to the corner and caught them just in time.

"Come. Come quickly," I pleaded. "There's been a hold-up in a shop just up the road. People have been robbed." The policemen glanced at the strange *mzungu* (white man) waving his arms about.

"Sorry, we can't," they replied, clearly unimpressed. "We are going to a meeting."

Batuk was more angry than shaken after his ordeal. He told me that he recognised the guns used in the hold-up as army or police issue. Batuk was a keen shooter and joined soldiers in competitions at the firing range. He was convinced that, in this case, the pistols were police issue.

The chilling assumption could be taken a stage further — the possibility that the gangsters were police, or ex-police themselves. In which case, Batuk could kiss goodbye to ever seeing his money again. Batuk was an Indian Kenyan, a leather merchant married to Clare, an English woman. They made an odd couple: He was as short as she was tall. They were totally devoted to each other and were well liked and respected members of the community. They were renowned for their organisational skills, particularly in the volunteer work they performed for Hillcrest Primary School where their sons and our daughter, Imogen, studied.

Well, it wasn't the end of the day for me. We drove home to Kileleshwa, where I wasted no time in pouring myself a triple scotch. Then, drink in hand, I climbed over the fence into my Welsh friend Kern Roberts' compound. Kern was washing his Pajero. He looked up with surprise and gestured pointedly at my drink.

"I don't usually drink before lunch," I ventured.

"A likely story," quipped Kern. "No, honestly," I said. "It's just that I have been held up at gunpoint and felt the need for a stiff drink."

Chapter 2

ONCE WERE LEOPARDS

Our African saga actually began in Nigeria and continued for nearly nine years in Kenya until my sudden expulsion from the country. Its genesis was in 1977 when, bored with my job as a senior sub-editor at *The Age* newspaper in Melbourne, Australia, I applied for the position of Director of the Nigerian Institute of Journalism.

Months later, after a delay probably due to the parlous state of the Nigerian telephone network, I got the call I had been waiting for. I would, said the caller, become the next director of the Institute. And my partner of two years, Diana Roberts, was of course coming with me.

But there was a hitch. The long-awaited divorce from my first wife had at last been set for hearing — the day before our flight to Lagos via Rome. The case went ahead however and a settlement was agreed. I was granted a divorce, with a decree nisi of three months. This meant Diana and I could not be married before our departure.

But no one had reckoned on the persuasive skills of my legal counsel.

The dialogue (or something very similar) went like this:

Counsel: "Your honour, I beg the court to abridge the decree."

Judge: "To when counsel?"

Counsel: "To this afternoon your honour."

Judge: (with growing irritation): "In heaven's name why?"

Counsel: "Because your honour, my client is leaving for Africa."

Judge: "So?"

Counsel: "Well, in that part of the world, your honour, they frown on unmarried couples and my client and his partner plan to marry tomorrow, just before the flight."

Judge: "Africa, you say?"

Counsel: "Yes, your honour, deepest, darkest Africa."

The request was granted and Family Law Court history made.

Hearing the news, Diana wasted no time in flipping through the pages of an old copy of *Encyclopaedia Britannica,* fixated on the section that dealt with Nigeria. "It says here," she said with awakening interest,"that leopards abound".

Until that moment she had been lukewarm, to say the least, with the prospect that we would soon be heading to the hot, steamy and most populous black nation on earth. But the thought of the thriving wildlife where leopards abounded had kindled other thoughts.

Our destination was the then capital of Lagos where I was to take up the directorship of the Institute, the principal training ground for the nation's newspaper reporters and broadcasters.

We were married the day we left Australia, flying via Rome (where we were robbed) for our two-day honeymoon. Such sudden departure had also created a crisis of identity as Diana had not had time to change the name in her passport from Roberts to Lawrence. This caused some embarrassment when we checked in at the Rome pension and handed our passports to the booking clerk. I had a sudden urge to explain:

"*Senora Roberts e la mia molie*," I offered in my sub–peasant Italian, blushing from ear to ear.

The clerk looked at the passport and at Diana, and then back to me, with a knowing smirk that said "just another dirty weekend". Then, without comment, he handed back our passports so we could complete booking formalities.

But this account is not about Rome and at the end of two days we found ourselves heading for the airport in a taxi at breakneck speed. I can vouch for the Kamikaze style of Italian drivers as two years later I had to dive to safety as a motorist in a narrow Florence street almost mowed me down. I shook my fist at him, shouting *mortachi toi* (death to yours). He laughed.

The pace at Rome's La Guardia international airport was frenetic, particularly at boarding time for the Lagos-bound Alitalia flight. The African passengers returning to Lagos were entering the plane with an eclectic array of luggage: cages of live fowl, huge boxes of Blue Omo washing powder and parcels of gifts for family and friends. The stewards and hostesses tried their best to stem the flow, but didn't always succeed. An African man struggled on board toting a large suitcase.

"Excuse me, sir," said the hostess, "only hand-luggage is allowed on this flight."

"Eh", said the man with dignity, "this is my briefcase. My suitcase is in the hold."

Faced with this distorted logic, the hostess gave up, but you had to admire Nigerian ingenuity. The flight was uneventful, except for one man who kept jumping up during ascent demanding "bring me cake!"

On the third demand, a male steward, with just a hint of malice, said: "You will sit down sir, and stay sitting down until the seatbelt sign goes off. Then I will bring you cake."

We touched down and disembarked under a scorching West African sun. It seemed to take an unconscionable time as the stream of people snaked out across the tarmac to the old airport building and immigration formalities. We must have been sweltering in the open and inside the building for a good two hours before we reached the Immigration desk. There was no air-conditioning because, typically, the power had failed. Huge bundles of plastic buckets and kettles, littered the area.

Summoning our happy-to-be-in-your-country smiles, we handed up our documents.

"No, you cannot come in," barked the officer with one bar on his epaulette. He snapped our passports shut and handed them back.

What? Can't come in! What is the man talking about?

"But but...." I stammered. "I have come here for two years to work. You must let us in."

"No, you cannot come in. You do not have entry visas and you do not have work visas."

"Look, we were told by your officials in Australia, that we didn't need them, that we could get them on our arrival here."

"I am sorry but you cannot enter Nigeria."

We looked at each other in dismay. We had come all this way and now were faced with the prospect of having to turn around and go back on the next available plane.

It was then that I had a sudden flash of inspiration. Reaching inside my inside jacket pocket I pulled out a neatly-typed letter.

It was my letter of appointment, signed by Alhaji Lateef Jakande, chairman of the Board of Governors of the Nigerian Institute of Journalism. Steadying myself and assuming a voice of authority, I said:

"I think you should read this" and handed the man the letter.

And read it he did. Every word. The size of my salary, conditions of employment and the perks that went with the job such as accommodation, car, domestic staff and membership of a club.

It was too much for the one-striper, who called up a two-striper, for a second opinion. The senior officer read the letter avidly while we sweated it out.

Abruptly he handed the letter back and warmly shook my hand.

"Welcome to Nigeria," he exclaimed with a beaming smile. And turning to Diana added: "And madam, may you have many babies here!"

Thus, on this surreal note, began our African adventure.

Chapter 3

APONGBONG STREET

After two days in recovery mode, I made my debut on a predictably hot, humid and steamy December day. The Institute was at the intersection of the aptly named Breadfruit and Apongbong Streets in downtown Lagos. The breadfruit had long gone for chop, that is, eaten, and Apongbong, fed by open drains, gave off malodorous smells.

The wooden, two-storey building, I was told, was a former mosque, but looked a little too dilapidated for that. On the ground floor were the classrooms and library. Upstairs was my office, my deputy's office, the office of the registrar and general administration. The power would go off, as regular as clockwork, at 8.30 — just as classes were starting — and would come back on at 4.30 just as classes were ending. Upstairs there was just enough power to cool the offices; downstairs there was nothing.

My designation was director and chief executive, answerable only to the board of governors through its redoubtable chairman, Alhaji Lateef Jakande. I also taught sub–editing and design to the senior class in the two-year diploma course. The Institute was financed chiefly by student fees and whatever could be raised through special seminars sponsored by industry and diplomatic sources. We taught all phases of journalism, including reporting, ethics, broadcasting, feature writing and shorthand. Other subjects were public relations, English, political science, sociology and economics. These were mostly taught by part-time lecturers.

My deputy director was Gabriel Ogunsekan, a typical knockabout journo who among other things had been a stringer for Reuters. Gabby had also been well-drilled in overseas courses and attachments in the United States and the UK. He was a solid and reliable backup for me and also shared some of the administrative load.

Among the regulars were Titus Ogunwale, who had written a book on African women's hairstyles and Ben Opolo who used to freak out Titus with a juju stone he kept in his pocket. Between them, they ran the three-month courses we regularly held for practising journalists.

The registrar was Ayo Ajayj and the bursar was Patrick Nwozor. And, praise the Lord, there was delightful and indispensible Sam, librarian and some-time driver. And Pius, messenger, front of door man and general factotum.

From the start I ran into the frustrations, breakdowns, shortages and challenges that were so much a feature of daily Lagos life. I had barely stepped foot inside the Institute building when I was besieged by reporters and TV cameramen demanding to know what I was going to do about a looming strike threat by students. I had absolutely no knowledge of what my interlocutor was talking about and offered a pathetic "well that's a leading question."

"Yes", said the man holding the microphone, "And that's why I am asking it!"

It was a day or two later when I ran into an even more pressing problem. John Lahey, my predecessor and colleague from my Melbourne newspaper *The Age,* had assured me that all his teaching materials were safely stowed in the registrar's safe. I was greatly relieved to hear this as I had never taught before and Lahey was a brilliant all-rounder: columnist, editor, wordsmith and layout expert. So things looked good. And so I thought — until I approached Ajayi and asked for the release of John's lecture notes. He looked at me blankly.

"What lecture notes?"

"The lecture notes John Lahey gave you custody of."

"I'm sorry, he didn't give me any lecture notes," said Ajayi.

I was shattered. My first lecture was due in a couple of days and I didn't have a shred to go on. Desperately I turned my desk drawers inside out. Nothing. I glanced around the room and there — lying in a dusty corner of the office — was an equally dusty part-completed John Lahey lecture. It was enough to get me going and I set to writing up my first lecture. Mafeking had been relieved.

On the day of the lecture the general office was still actually cyclostyling my notes on an ancient Gestetner machine for distribution to the students. I was as nervous as a kitten as I faced the 60 black students who squeezed sardine-like into the narrow gutted room.

The classroom abutted a laneway and passers-by would sometimes thrust their arms through the Louvre windows and shake hands with the students. Even hold a conversation with them.

My knees were knocking as I launched into my lecture and I did not relax until the time came for questions.

"Any questions?" I asked.

A hand shot up.

"Yessir. How old are you sir?"

The class laughed. The ice was broken.

Next day I had my introduction at first-hand to the Nigerian Electric Power Authority — or NEPA as it is more commonly referred to. I had barely begun my lecture when the power suddenly went off.

"Ah, Nepa don quench," shouted the class in classic West Coast pidgin. Enough was enough, as Maggie Thatcher might have said. The intense heat was hard enough to take, but without an air-conditioner, it was unbearable. Something had to be done. So, after class I called out for Pius.

"I'm coming suh, I'm coming suh," Pius called back and immediately scuttled off in the opposite direction. This was something new, but it translated into "Coming sir, I'll be there in a tick." A few ticks later Pius re-emerged in my office.

"You sent for me suh."

"Yes, Pius. Nepa don quench again and we've simply got to do something about it."

"You can't beat Nepa sir. *Nah be so*?"

"*Be so*. But I want you to come with me to the shops to buy a portable generator."

Thus the Institute became the proud owner of a 3.5KV generator, which would be enough to turn the ceiling fans in the ground floor classrooms when NEPA quenched.

Alas, this was not the end of the problem. First we had to get petrol — and that, it transpired, proved to be no mean feat. When Pius went to the petrol station, armed with a jerry can, a suspicious attendant refused to supply him. To prove the petrol was really for a generator at the NIJ, he said Pius had to bring the school bus to the station to make the collection.

So here we had the absurd situation of taking a bus meant to transport 32 students with the sole objective of filling a four-gallon jerry can with petrol. Of course, it all seemed worthwhile when, to the relieved cheers of the class, it burst into life and the fans wafted in a cooling breeze. After that classes went along smoothly to the comforting whirr of the fans, until....

......splutter, splutter....the generator stopped.

"Pius," I yelled.

"Coming suh."

"Pius, the generator has broken down"

"No suh, it just *don* run out of petrol suh."

"Yes Pius, but you must get more petrol *before* it runs out."

"How do we know suh when it is going to run out?"

A fair question, but I had the solution and shopped around until I found wooden ruler, the sort that all school students used to have. I then measured it up against the generator's fuel tank and cut a notch in it a few inches from the bottom. It made a great dip-stick.

"Now Pius, when the petrol gets below this mark it's time to go out and buy more."

"Yes suh. I will do this."

All went well for the next few lectures. then the petrol don quench. Again!

"Pius, I told you that when the petrol gets below.....

"Yes suh, I forgot suh."

Pius was actually the salt of the earth, a good-natured man who seldom complained about his workload. Except for the trekking, that is. As the NIJ's telephone seldom, if ever, worked, it meant that Pius, as chief messenger and general factotum, had to trek miles around the bustling city delivering important missives. If things got really urgent, then Sam, librarian and part-time driver, doubled up to share the load. But it was Pius who did most of the trekking, through the traffic-jammed streets and the dripping humidity.

Pius put up with his trekking burden until one day he'd had enough and began lobbying for an office motorbike. As a previous machine, as Pius termed it, had been stolen, the NIJ was at first reluctant to buy another one. However, at last we relented and Pius became the proud custodian of a two-stroke motorbike and was soon zipping cheerfully through the streets of Lagos.

Now one of Pius' duties was to go to the post office each morning and collect the mail bag. He would ride up to the PO and securely lock the bike to the steel rack provided for the purpose. The lock was big and the chain heavy.

Then. Suddenly. High drama.

A crestfallen Pius came back late to the office one morning to report his precious motorbike stolen. He had stepped out of the post office with his mailbag and stared in disbelief at where the bike had been.

We were not amused.

"Didn't you secure the bike to the steel stand, Pius?"

"Yes suh, but the thief man *don* took it too."

"What the stand too, Pius?"

"Yes suh, he took the machine, the chain and the stand!"

So Pius went back to trekking.

In fact, this was a situation that spread, like some alien disease across the length and breadth of Lagos. This combined, with the dreaded go-slow traffic snarl that plagued the city, meant it was usually much quicker to deliver a message by hand than by any other means. Trekkers therefore performed a valuable service for their employers.

And my office telephone, which could have eased Pius' burden, reposed on my desk, a useless unwanted ornament. In disgust I threw it under the visitors' couch next to the desk. There it lay until a day in late March 1979 when, with a loud series of rings, it burst into life. I sat bolt upright with shock. It was if a bomb had gone off. The students' magazine *Peep* reported the miracle thus:

Hello. Is that 637743?

Yes.

Can I speak with Mr Lawrence?

Speaking.

"Thus the telephone line of the Institute awoke from its slumber. The line had been dead for nearly 14 months." Then, unfortunately, it went straight back to sleep again.

However many more minor problems were solved through the simple expedient of going out into the street and shouting for help.

"Is there a carpenter around here?"

Doors would fly open and citizens pour out. "I am the carpenter!" a dozen voices would reply. Or, similarly,

"I need a plumber."

"I am the plumber!"

Cecil B de Mille would have had a field day with this cast.

Loftus Harris, the deputy Australian Trade Commissioner at the time, recounted to Diana a hilarious conversation he had with a woman on the Lagos telephone exchange. Loftus was trying to ring his mother in Australia.

Loftus: I would like to place a call to Australia.

Exchange: Who are you calling?

Loftus: I am *calling* number xyzxyz in Australia.

Exchange: But who are you calling?

Loftus (puzzled): I am calling my mother in Australia.

Exchange (a little tensely): Who are ***you*** calling?

Loftus: My mother, Mrs Harris, on number xyzxyz in ...

Exchange: I asked you who are **YOU** calling?

Loftus (the penny dropping): Oh! Who am I?

Exchange: Yes. Who are you!

Loftus: I am Loftus Harris and I am calling....

Exchange: putting your call through now Mr Loftus.

Chapter 4

WATCHING THE NIGHT

Our home for the next two years was a two-bedroom flat in New Ikoyi, once part of Ikoyi Island, but landfill and a new bridge network now connected it to old Ikoya and on to Lago Island and the CBD. The journey by car took maybe half an hour, but a few years earlier the route was a nightmare. Klaus Roos, Director of the Nigerian branch of the Goethe Institute, told me it was not uncommon for motorists to take more than four hours for the trip.

The journey was exacerbated by the infamous and aptly named *Go-Slow,* which then, and now, paralysed so much of Lagos roads. Motorists, said Klaus, were even known to have died, as they sat in their cars, hours on end, in intense heat waiting for a break in the traffic. He recalls his own frustration, lucky to make it to his office in under two hours.

Klaus and his wife Elisabeth made a charming couple and were our nearest neighbours — living directly opposite across the landing from our own flat. Their houseman was a handsome and extremely polite young Nigerian, who, according to Klaus, looked smarter than he actually was. For some time Elisabeth had noticed that their bottle of gin had been tasting weaker and weaker, but had not been getting lower than the level they had marked with a pencil.

Finally Elisabeth said: "Klaus, this is not gin. It is water!"

The houseman, confronted with the evidence, confessed. But he wasn't sacked. He had otherwise good qualities and, besides, they liked him.

Our flat was moderately comfortable, but the furniture was sparse and decidedly PWD (Public Works Department). One of the flat's saving graces was the balcony overlooking the compound's garden where I would sit, whisky in one hand, half corona cigar in the other, watching the mouse-sized bats skitter across the twilight sky as they foraged for insects. I would come inside only when the squadrons of dive-bombing malarial mosquitoes interrupted my musings.

The worst part was the frequent lack of water in the large tank that serviced the six flats in the block. When it ran dry, as it often did, the only way we could bathe or take a shower, was to fetch water from a distant source and haul it up to the second floor in jerry cans. This arduous task fell to John, our seldom-complaining steward. We solved the problem — or thought we had — by buying water by the tanker-load. But there was catch: As soon as other residents in our block realised we had water, they would turn on their taps and fill up baths, basins and saucepans. It was a modern twist on the old novelty ditty:

"There's a hole in the bucket, dear Liza, dear Liza, A hole."

"Well mend it dear Henry, dear Henry. Mend it."

We mended, but didn't reckon on the lightning reflexes of our neighbours. John was an *Igbo* (also referred to as *Ibo*[2]), the people from the eastern states. He was a zealous worker, no more so than in the way he tackled the odd blowfly that buzzed its way indoors. John would shoot it with a can of Doom fly-spray and follow it down in its death spiral, blazing away until it hit the floor and buzzed around like a top on its bottom. Whereupon he would empty the rest of the can, adding new meaning to the term road kill.

"I think he's dead, John," I would say.

John took the compliment with good grace.

In new Ikoyi, as elsewhere in greater Lagos, air-conditioners and ceiling fans were not just desirable, they were essential if you wanted any quality of life. Even then, everything depended on the unpredictable NEPA and when it *quenched,* as it often did, you felt it. Sometimes it would *quench* at night. Comforted by the hum of the air-conditioner, you would fall into a deep sleep. Then NEPA would *quench*, as the locals would say, and the power would fail. It was the silence that would awaken you, followed by a trickle of sweat.

It was never cold in Lagos. Often on a Sunday evening Diana and I would fantasise when we saw leaves falling outside and imagine it was snowing. Only to be hit with a fetid blast of tropical air if we stepped outside. However, the locals *did* feel the cold when once a year a phenomenon called the *Harmattan* arrived.[1]

This happens in December when Sahara Desert sand, stirred up by seasonal winds, partially blots out the sun. In the big UTC store in downtown Lagos, the display-window signs urged customers:

"Beat the Harmattan. Buy your beanies, blankets and overcoats here."

During Harmattan the sun shone through like a sickly disc. The day-time temperature dropped by a few degrees, but everything is relative and to anyone but the locals it was still hot. Bloody hot.

The only other irritant in our flat life was, I suppose, the need to be more careful with food hygiene. For example, not only did we boil our drinking water, but first we had to filter it to remove any suspicious-looking solids. Some expats, however, were paranoid, going so far as to wash lettuce leaves in Milton. Others didn't quite trust the local toilet paper, bringing their own supplies from their home countries.

Security was not a problem — except on one occasion when I went downstairs to the car port to get my small red Peugeot. Keys in hand, I was about to drive to work, when I pulled up short. Where my car was always parked was empty space and sitting in that empty space was a middle-aged African whom I presumed to be the nightwatchman.

"Who are you," I asked him. "And where is my car?"

"I am the watchnight," he replied.

"You mean the nightwatch," I corrected him.

"No masta, I am the watchnight. I watch the night. The thief man come in the night and he steal your motor. "

"Did he now? And why didn't you stop him?"

"He say masta, you *don* shut your mouth or I will cut your throat."

The wretched man, visibly cowed, made a convincing swipe from ear to ear across his neck. Fair enough. A car can always be replaced, but not a throat.

Odd things happened during our time in Nigeria, but none so

odd as the scene that took place on the morning after our arrival. We had barely stirred from our slumbers, bleary eye and more than a little jet-lagged, when the front door bell rang.

I opened the door to be confronted by an African in flowing traditional dress, clutching off all things a battered Gladstone bag.

Wasting no time, he inquired: Are you Mr Lawrence?" And for good measure "Mr John Lawrence?"

"Yes, but who are you and how do you know my name?"

"I am the tailor, masta. I am Mr Lawal and I am bringing you hot drinks every week, sir."

Bizarre thoughts raced through my head. This tailor, of whom I have never heard, is bringing me hot drinks. Coffee, tea and Bonox? The mystery partly unravelled as a beaming Mr Lawal, the tailor, opened his Gladstone bag to reveal three bottles of White *'Horsch'* (White Horse) Scotch whisky, three bottles of brandy and three bottles of Gordon's gin.

"Ah", I said with surprise and delight, "those sorts of hot drinks!"

All very welcome, but how did Mr Lawal know my name? How did he know where I lived and how did he know that I was partial to a wee drop? Mr Lawal must have been reading my mind.

"The other masta sent me," he said, as if that were more than enough enlightenment. "The masta upstairs."

Mr Lawal pointed to the flat above. It made no sense.

"Who is the other masta that sent you?" I probed patiently.

"The other masta, Mr Rick Aspinal."

The penny dropped. Back in Melbourne, John Lahey, my predecessor, had told me that Rick, a UNESCO communications expert with diplomatic status, would make a useful contact. Furthermore, he had advised Rick that I was coming and that I "held a glass very nicely". And the upstairs bit? That was Mr Lawal's way of saying that Masta Aspinal lived in a flat just like ours, albeit a good kilometre or two from where we lived.

So, without further ado, Mr Lawal, tailor and purveyor of spirituous liquors, unloaded his fare.

"Every week," he said, "I bring you hot drinks. If you are not home, I leave them outside your door." With that Mr Lawal got on his bicycle, Gladstone bag on the carrier rack, and peddled off to his next port of call.

It was a neat arrangement, but, although we could more than handle the White Horsch, to consume the rest would have challenged the most diligent of dipsomaniacs. So we asked Mr Lawal to scale down the order a tad. He looked somewhat disappointed when we put our request. Our reputation had gone down a peg or two!

We enjoyed Rick's company — up to a point. Rick had a strong background in radio and had played had a big part in setting up broadcasting facilities in several Third World countries. He was debonair, a fastidious cook, and a witty raconteur. He had a habit of dropping around late at night to chew the fat and enjoy more than a wee dram or two of our scotch.

Before you knew it we had discussed Nigerian and world affairs at length and polished off a bottle of Mr Lawal's White Horsch. However that was not the end of it as Rick, before making his goodbyes, he would say: "Well, let's have a lucky last" and another bottle would be opened. This would be followed by an "absolute bloody last", an "absolute bloody, bloody last" and an" absolute, bloody fucking last". Mr Lawal knew something when he offloaded his initial order.

It got to the stage when if we heard a car pull into the compound's driveway late at night, we would peep out the window and Diana would urge:

"Quick, I think it's Rick" and we would draw the curtains and douse the lights. Then when Rick stomped up the stairs and rang the doorbell, we would lie doggo and pretend to be fast asleep.[2]

Chapter 5

DINNER FOR THREE

One of my lecturers tried to wheedle his way into my good books during my early days at the Institute. Ben Opolo wasted almost no time in inviting Diana and myself to dinner. Hard to refuse when you are the new boy on the block and getting to know the ropes. So I said: "Sure Ben, we would love to have dinner at your place."After work, with me driving and Ben describing the passing scene, we headed for his home on the mainland.

In those days, driving anywhere in Lagos was an adventure: pothole impossible to evade, kamikaze drivers on the road and the dreadful mini-buses called *danfos.* Rules of the road meant nothing to the drivers and touts who operated them. There was a story going around in diplomatic circles about the danfo driver who found his way blocked during one of the Lagos go-slows — traffic jams that resulted in absolute gridlock.

Danfo drivers thought nothing of turning two lanes into three or even for. Often they drove on the footpaths as well. On this occasion, the danfo mounted the footpath and struck an elderly male pedestrian, No apology. No sorry for hurting you sir, are you all right? Can I take you to hospital? Just a torrent of abuse for being in the danfo's way, punctuated by a few well-timed kicks to the injured man's body.

Apart from such unruly scenes, there were also the roadside rubbish dumps, as ubiquitous as the potholes. It was not uncommon to see a huge mound of rubbish beside the road and atop of it a sign that read NO RUBBISH DUMPING. And only the top of the sign visible. In time this sign would be swallowed up by another mound on top of the existing one and the sign pulled out and stuck on top of the new pile.

About half the way to the house, Ben asked us to stop outside an off-licence shop.

"Do you and madam drink wine?" he asked. "Yes, Ben, we do drink wine."

"What sort of wine do you drink," he inquired.

"Red wine, "I said.

"And you, madam. What sort of wine do you drink."

"White wine," said Diana. Ben disappeared into the off-licence and returned in a few minutes clutching two brown paper bags. We drove on through more depressing urban sights until we came at last to Ben's house — and stepped into a furnace. If it was hot in the tropical early night air, the heat was even more intense inside the house.

Ben apologised. "I'm sorry it's so hot," he said, "but the air-conditioning has broken down because the electricity is off. And we can't open the windows because the mosquitoes will come in." Of course, due to the electricity blackout, the fridge was not working. Any thoughts of a refreshing cool drink of water were out too.

But Ben had prepared for dinner. So we sat down to a meal of curried chicken, served up by a girl servant. She could have been no more than 10 or 11. If there were a Mrs Opolo, she certainly made no appearance. Anyway, we started to eat, making stilted small talk.

Beads of perspiration formed on our foreheads and became drops of sweat.

At one point we were interrupted by a squawk. Followed a few minutes later by another squawk. Then another. The squawks seemed to be coming from under our table.

"What have you got there Ben?" I ventured. "It sounds like a hen or rooster."

"Yes it is," replied Ben without a shred of embarrassment and added:

"Shut up fowl!"

I took a quick glance under the table and, sure enough, uncaged was a scrawny young rooster, crowing and crapping merrily away.

"Tomorrow's dinner," I whispered to Diana out of the back of my hand.

When we were about half way through our dinner, Ben remembered the wine, which he produced with a flourish.

We were like stunned mullets as Ben first poured Diana's "wine" into a 10-ounce tumbler. Gin! Pure gin. Sans tonic. Sans ice. Stunned as she was, Diana had the good grace and manners to take a cautious sip. But she couldn't hide the grimace and Ben noticed it.

"Diana, you don't like your wine. You said you liked white wine."

Diana tried to explain the difference between wine and spirits, but made no impression. He then produced and poured my "red wine" into a tumbler. Dubonet! Warm undiluted dubonet. Manfully I downed the glass in a series of quick gulps.

Clearly Ben was no sommelier. Diana was staring mournfully at her "white wine". To save face for our host, I then picked up her glass of warm gin and downed it, too.

For embarrassment, the wine fiasco could only be compared with the al fresco dinner party that the Australian High Commission hosted after the annual tennis challenge. The challenge was between Australian and Canada. Unlike in the real world, Canada had won 17 out the last 18 contests. Guests were seated at tables on the lawn and separated by large pots of exotic plants.

The night was hot but fine, accompanied by hordes of malarial mosquitoes. The party was informal, as evidenced by the casks of Australian red and white wine that graced the tables. There was only one thing wrong: the casks had spent weeks, possibly months, sitting in the tropical sun on the Apapa wharf.

Whether by neglect, bureaucratic indifference or failure to pay a bribe was not the point. As all wine lovers know, two things are inimical to any vintage: movement and temperature fluctuation. This consignment had had a surfeit of both. Put simply, the white wine had oxidised. When the chardonnay was poured into the glass, the colour resembled pale ale and tasted a bit like it too.

Embarrassment became acute as High Commissioner Kevin Flanagan walked by the tables intoning "Good evening. And how are you enjoying our fine Australian wines."

"Fine, Ambassador, absolutely tops," they lied convincingly — and then, when he was gone, tipped their wine into the handily placed flower pots.

Chapter 6

THE THIEF MAN COMES

The Australian High Commission provided a social lifeline for us as well as employment for Diana, who was in charge of archives after being cleared by the Australian Security and Intelligence Commission (ASIO). It was probably, too, a bit of stimulation for permanent staff to have someone new in a renowned hardship post. It was, to boot, one of the few entertainment outlets available. One heard tales of housewives, the trailing spouses, who spent bored listless hours lazing around swimming pools. There was gossip about affairs and marriage breakdowns. And there was often substance in the gossip.

We quickly made friends with the High Commission staff, which formed a network for making friends with Australians and people from other countries in business, agriculture and education. And we were grateful to be unofficially included on the tail end of meat, cheese and wine orders from Australia.

As mentioned in the previous chapter, the High Commissioner during our stay was the veteran diplomat Kevin Flanagan. The Trade Commissioner was John Lightfoot and his deputy was the affable giant Loftus Harris who provided us with moments of great hilarity. Loftus went on to carve out a brilliant career at home and abroad.

We first met Loftus at a masked whisky tasting in the apartment of Alex Brooking, an ambitious young third secretary with a bent for entertaining. It was a blind tasting, the sort where the bottles are masked and identified by number only. Each guest was given a piece of paper and a pencil with instructions to guess the brand, give it a score out of 10 and write a comment.

In all, there were about 18 bottes of single malt and blended scotches like Johnnie Walker red label and Chivas Regal. A bottle of sherry and a bottle of water were thrown in for good measure. After a few nips of the good stuff, it was hard for some to tell if they were drinking whisky, sherry, tea or water. Loftus warmed to the challenge and got really fixated on one drop, taking a good swig rather than a temperate single sip.

"Mmmmmmm" said Loftus, before reluctantly releasing the bottle to the next guest, "not quite sure. Need another sip to compare." Loftus, we were told, did not report for work next day.

Some of the diplomats had already moved to a new sandy estate being developed on Victoria Island, among them Loftus. Loftus used to scoot about in a Honda Civic — a ridiculously small car for such a large man. He tells the story of backing out of his driveway, when there was loud bang. A cyclist had collided with his car. Soon an angry crowd had gathered, banging on the car door and blaming him for the accident.

It was getting ugly until Loftus slowly started, amid oohs and ahs, to unfold his big frame from the Honda. In a masterful display of sangfroid, Loftus turned the incident to his advantage.

"I did not hit this cyclist," he said, pointing to the car door. See. Look at that dent. His head hit *my* car!"

The mood changed.

"Ooh, yes. He *has* hit your car, the crowd chanted — and vented their anger on the wretched man.

In those days, the estate was in its formative stage and the block next to Loftus was vacant and overgrown with long grass. Enter now Loftus' nightwatchman, a fierce-looking Tuareg, complete with lethal-looking sword hanging by his side.

On this occasion Loftus had been out late and had returned home to find Musa still standing guard. "Morning Musa," said Loftus. "Everything go all right during the night?"

"Yessir, no problem. But the thief man come."

"The thief man?" queried Loftus raising an eyebrow.

"Yessir, no problem. I cut off his head," said the nightwatchman miming the decapitation with a vicious sweep of his sword hand.

"What did you do with the head Musa?"

"No problem sir. I threw it into the block next door."

I next saw Loftus some years later when he was stationed in Hong Kong. His apartment was high up on the Peak. Loftus ushered me onto the balcony to view the spectacular scene. Way below the night lights twinkled across the city. It was a bit like a Jesus moment. Breathtaking.

Loftus Harris went on to stake out a distinguished and decorated career[1], rising to assistant trade commissioner and senior trade commissioner in embassies in West Africa, Asia, Scandinavia, Europe and the Middle East. For 10 years, until late 2007 he was Director of the Department of State and Regional Development in New South Wales and before that

Director-General of the Queensland Department of the Premier. He was a special trade representative to the Middle East and India for the Queensland Government. His is an AM in the Order of Australia.

Chapter 7

THE TYRE SLASHERS

Life on the streets of Lagos was always chaotic. But if you took prudent precautions, ignored daily hazards of touts, beggars, pot-holes and kamikaze traffic, you could get by. The key to survival was a sense of humour. If you didn't possess one, you might as well pack up and go home to comfy nine-to-five workplace existence.

Almost from day one, we were amused at being greeted with shouts of *OYIBO, OYIBO* in that sing-song Yoruba accent. In the market place, in the shops. Everywhere it was *Oyibo, Oyibo*.

When Diana, an excellent horsewoman, rode the police horses over the Falomo Bridge to the Victoria Island beachfront, a dozen or so excited children would chase after her calling out *Oyibo, Oyibo*. It was obviously a unique sight for them: a strange white woman on top of a great chestnut steed.

(The offer to ride the police horse followed a conversation Diana had with a retired deputy police commissioner at our main watering hole — the Ikoyi Cub. His offer was joyfully accepted.)

We soon learned the meaning or meanings of the word

Oyibo. Our friend Jane Loudon, a journalist attached to the International Institute of Tropical Agriculture at Ibadan, says *Oyibo* means "peeled like a banana", the way all of us would look if we were skinned. The word is common to pidgin, Yoruba and Igbo and is used in a fun way to describe white people.

According to the Nairaland Forum it translates from the Yoruba as "peeled skin" or "skinless". So Jane's banana analogy is pretty well spot on. Urban Dictionary says *Oyibo* can also be used mockingly to call out a Nigerian wannabe trying to act above his station in life, or putting on airs. In Australian slang, it would mean "bunging on side".

You also needed a sense of humour when confronted by the blackmail tactics of parking touts. Parking was a problem for *Oyibos* in Lagos, but not so much for the locals who parked their cars and *danfos* (mini passenger buses) in any vacant or almost vacant spot. On the road. On the roundabout. On the kerb. On the footpath. Wherever.

An Oyibo, fluking a good spot, would often be approached by a tout demanding "money for minding your car". The street smart would sigh and hand over a few *kobo* or *naira*. Motorists who stood on their dignity and dismissed the touts with a few well-chosen words, would return to find their tyres slashed.

Even this could have a funny side. Once in a while, seeking breathing space away from Lagos, we would drive 57 kilometres for a swim and a picnic at Badagry on the Atlantic coast near the Republic of Benin. On this occasion, we had driven up a grassy slope to park within sight of a splendid stretch of beach and the rolling waves of the Atlantic.

Before we had even stopped, a horde of young boys swarmed

over the car, bouncing on the bonnet and tapping on the windows. We stepped out to a chorus of hopeful shouts:

"I will mind your car."

"Please sir, I am the best, sir".

I looked the bunch over. Most of them were in a broad age group of about eight to 12.

One boy stood out. He was about 14 or 15 and head and shoulders above the rest. "Who are you. What's your name?" I asked.

"My name is Thompson sir," he replied politely." I no go slash your tyres."

"Thompson," I said. "You're my man. Guard my car with your life."

When we returned a couple of hours later, Thompson, true to his word, was still guarding the car. We *dashed* (tipped) him handsomely.

Another time we jumped into our friend Scott McTaggart's motorboat and cruised from the broad reaches of Five Cowrie Creek to where a spit of land separates the creek from the Atlantic Ocean. Here the Atlantic drops away sharply from the shoreline. No place for safe swimming, but when a fishing boat rode the breakers in, we helped pull it ashore.

Our reward? A bucketful of delicious blue swimmer crabs. We found an old iron container half-buried in the sand and boiled up the crabs in sea water. Soon Diana, Scott's wife Narelle, Scott and myself were feeding our faces on one of the most memorable of crab meals.

Five Cowrie Creek is actually a small river, which is fed by the Lagos Lagoon, the largest body of fresh water in Lagos, and empties into Lagos Harbour. It is a popular real estate site and substantial houses line its sandy shores. But its shifting tidal movements sometimes hide dark secrets. Long-term residents tell of times when skeletons have suddenly appeared at low tide. On one celebrated occasion residents reported to police that a body had been washed up on the edge of their property. The police were not having anything to with it.

"It's a job for the water police," they said.

Predictably, the water police said: "No, it is on your property. Clearly a job for the land police."

And so the argument went back and forth. In the end the land police won by a technical knockout and, using a long pole, pushed the body back into the downstream current.

You get your pleasures in the most unlikely places in Lagos. Such was the case when we went to an outdoor movie at our club, the Ikoyi Club. The night was predictably hot; the mosquitoes were out in droves and moths, insects and the odd bat flitted around light from the projector.

The film, as I remember it, was about a beautiful young woman wrongfully accused and tried for murder. She was found guilty and sentenced to death. Then just when she was about to swing for the crime, a loud African voice split the night air: "AH! BRITISH JUSTICE!" Of course, the pretty young girl got a last-minute reprieve.

Some weekends we would head off by ourselves, or with friends, to our local beach, the famous Bar Beach, a pleasant sun-baking spot on Victoria Island and safe to swim there if you stayed in the shallows. Beyond that, the Atlantic shoreline fell away sharply, creating a strong tow and rip that made swimming dangerous for all but the strongest swimmers. Lifesavers were always pulling swimmers, African and expatriates alike, from deeper water.

Bar Beach also had a more sinister reputation as a popular site for public executions. The unfortunate criminals, armed robbers and coup plotters, would be tied to stakes in front of 44-gallon drums. Often it would be a job lot and several at a time would face the firing squad. Before and after pictures were often published in the local press. The Federal Military Government reacted harshly to crime. In 1984, five years after we had left the country, it issued a series of new decrees. They were listed, as follows, in the *Nigerian Tribune* of 26 July 1984:

Arson	death by firing squad
Tampering with oil pipelines	death by firing squad
Tampering with telephone cables	death by firing squad
Illegal importation of mineral ore	death by firing squad
Possessing counterfeit currency	death by firing squad
Selling cocaine	death by firing squad
Buying/inhaling/drinking cocaine	death by firing squad

Perhaps, in a proportional sense, the harshest punishment of all was 21 years jail for cheating at exams. Against this, "destruction of highways" brought a mere five years in prison.

However, back to horse-riding and a delightful neo-colonial touch. Their surnames names are long forgotten, but among the many people we met were the two Peters, British male architects who had been in the country for 29 and 22 years respectively. They lived in a grand double-storey mansion. The upper floor balcony was lined with some of the finest antiques we had seen outside of museums: Benin bronzes, Yoruba tribal wood carvings, brass statuary and other priceless artwork.

But their prized possessions lived and breathed. Our hosts opened a door and there on their masters' beds reclined five beautifully groomed and pampered saluki dogs. The salukis were soon put to the test. The 6am riding/driving party consisted of the two architects, a husband and wife couple and Diana. The middle-aged architects drove the Suzuki while the salukis loped alongside. Sykes from the Polo Club in Ikoyi brought up the horses and Diana and the couple saddled up.

The salukis, among the fastest dog breeds in the world, had great staying power but took it in turns to hitch a ride. For two hours the riders cantered along Bar Beach. Then they would take a break and open the lovingly packed thermos of dry martinis — and, refreshed, canter back.

Chapter 8

ENTER THE PRINCE

In hindsight, I don't know why we hired him. The Prince — perhaps he had another name, but I can't recall — came to the Institute seeking a job as the director's driver. He claimed not only to be of royal descent, but to have been personal driver to generals in India and Burma during the Second World War. He carried no testimonial or proof of this, but it could well have been correct.

The Nigerians played a significant, and at times a heroic, and largely unsung, role fighting against the Japanese not only in India, but in Burma as well. In fact, they made up more than half of the 90,000 West African soldiers under the British in the Burma campaign.[1]

But royalty? In a land of 521 languages and dozens of royal titles, where did the Prince's lineage originate? Among the traditional rulers were the Oba (common in several states) the Obi, the Igwe, the Eze, the Oomi, the Emirs, and Alakes and the Shehu. And many, many more. Also, the Prince was rather elderly, but sprightly enough to engage my attention. Besides, there was my vanity. I rather fancied the notion of being driven around by a prince. Deal done. Sealed with a handshake.

An important role for the director of the NIJ was showing the flag, so to speak, at the newspapers and radio and television stations that sent their young journalists to the Institute for training. In the late 1970s there were 19 States in Nigeria, most of which had all three forms of media, plus flourishing government information offices. To get around all of them in a year was almost impossible, so we had to cherry pick. Today, with 36 States, the job would have been even more difficult.

So one day in 1978, the Prince at the wheel, Diana and I set off on a tour of the east, stopping and sleeping at Enugu before swinging down to oil-rich Port Harcourt, capital of Rivers State, and then, via Onitsha, on to the ancient city of Benin in Benue State.

In Port Harcourt we did our flag-showing bit, chatting with newspaper and television executives before resuming the journey. Or that was our intention. All went well for the first 15 minutes — and then the troubles started, sparking a series of events that threatened our lives.

We were admiring the passing scene, pointing out aspects of interest. One feature I remember well was an idyllic river scene where local women, stripped to the waist, were washing clothes. Vigorously dunking their garments into the stream and then beating them against rocks. But after some minutes, we again saw the same women washing their clothes in the river. Again and again.

"Prince," I ventured, "I think we are going around in circles."

"What," shouted the Prince, his voice rising sharply. There was an edge of aggression in it. "What are you saying sir"?

"Well, we have just passed this spot by the river for about the third time. I recognise the same women washing their clothes. We need to get onto the road that leads to Benin City."

There are some things you can say to a man, and some things you can't. Among the things you can't say, or even suggest, are that he is a lousy lover, a poor drinker or a bad driver. The Prince obviously thought I was casting aspersions on his driving skills.

"I am the best driver. Very best driver," he screamed. "I know every road in Nigeria like the back of my hand. I was number one driver during the war. I drove the general everywhere in India."

"Yes, I understand Prince, but we really do need to get on the right road."

Just when I thought the Prince was about to have an apoplectic fit, he found the opening to the Benin road. But the troubles and the Prince's temper had only started. From being a reasonably sedate driver, the Prince put his foot down and the speedometer needle went ballistic.

Diana, in the back seat with me, was having a fit of her own.

"For Christ's sake, John, tell him to slow down."

"Prince," I yelled, "*don't* go so fast."

The Prince's response was to up the speed a few more notches.

"Prince," I yelled again, "*don't* go so fast." The Prince's lead foot pushed the speedo to new heights.

Diana was the first to twig. "He thinks you are telling him to go faster,"she cried. "Tell him to slow down."

Why didn't I think? In West African pidgin *don* means *do* or *does*. So the Prince, thinking he is hearing *don* instead of *don't* went faster and faster. By this time we were up that well-known creek without a paddle. We were seriously worried.

"For fuck's sake Prince, slow down. Stop the bloody car."

And that is what the Prince did next. Stopped. Suddenly. We were almost propelled into the front seat. Worse was to come.

The Prince, now out his mind with rage, jumped out of the car and started shouting to passing traffic about the dreadful white man in the car. Then he turned his attention to God, cupping hand to ear and exclaiming:

"What is that Lord? What is that you are saying? Yes, that is right, the white man is....

It was then that I noticed the *panga* (machete) beside the driver's seat. Here we were in the middle of the jungle and our fate in the hands of a deranged driver. So I changed tack, pleading with the Prince to get back in the car, and delivering the biggest *mea culpa* of my life.

"I apologise Prince, "I said and then rather pathetically added "If the white man has offended the black man he apologises. I am very, very sorry Prince, but please, please get back in the car. And so he did. Finally. Not exactly mollified, but the edge had gone from his anger.

We motored on in awkward silence, aiming to make Benin City, nearly 300 kilometres away, before nightfall. The countryside changed from thick jungle-like banana plantations to more open country, revealing the rich agriculture of Rivers State: yam, cassava, coconut and maize.

Bye and bye the Prince noticed a woman selling bush rats by the side of the road. He stopped the car and sauntered over. The giant African rat (*Cricetomys sp Ansorgei*) is nothing like our scavenging, disease-carrying rat (*rattus rattus*). It is the size of a good sized rabbit, growing to almost 1.3 kilograms and is found all over the African continent. A Nigerian expert, Mojisola Oyarekua from the Institute of Science and Technology, says it is especially delicious. Money for weight, it is more expensive than beef or fish. You can eat it, he adds, roasted, boiled or dry.[2]

The Prince examined the rats on offer and bought two, making the mistake (as we shall see later) by tying them to the manifold of a very hot engine. Somewhat appeased by now, he again stopped a few kilometres further on and bought three large yams — one for each of his three wives. It is amazing how quickly the thought of food changes a man's mood. A factor in the bizarre behaviour of the Prince might have been his fear of people in the eastern states, who, he believed, were possessed by black magic.

So, with relieved passengers and a happier Prince, we resumed our journey to Benin City arriving shortly before dark. As was the custom with drivers, the Prince went off to find his own accommodation, and we booked in to our hotel. My parting shot to the Prince was: "Now Prince make sure you are back here no later than eight in the morning. We have a long day's drive back to Lagos ahead of us."

"Yes sir," said the Prince equably, and went off to find digs for the night.

Chapter 9

EXIT THE PRINCE

We arose at seven and ate a hearty English-style breakfast. Then we packed, paid our bill and waited for the Prince to arrive. We weren't exactly checking our watches every two or three minutes, but eight o'clock came and went and a certain tension started to play at our nerves. Nine came around. The tension was palpable. Where is the prince?

We didn't have mobile phones in those days, so we could not ring the prince. We didn't know where the hell our driver was. Time passed. Still no Prince. We contemplated ringing the institute for help. But the NIJ telephone seldom, if ever, worked. Then, to our great relief, the Prince at 10 o'clock, marched, or should I say, staggered in. Drunk. The Prince was drunk. Very, very, very drunk. The conversation that ensued was not for delicate ears, but expletives toned down, it went like this:

"Prince, where the bloody hell have you been?"

"I am reporting for duty as directed," he slurred.

"Like hell you are. We agreed you would be here by eight. It is now 10.30."

The Prince was unperturbed. "I drive right now," he protested.

"No you damn well can't. Not while you are drunk. You would kill us all."

The Prince bridled.

"I am not drunk. I will drive you to Lagos. I will show you."

With that, the Prince jumped into the car. And reversed. Straight into a shiny new Mercedes Benz. Top of the range stuff. There was a loud bang and guests came running out of the hotel, including the owner of the Mercedes.

I forget his name, but he was obviously a big shot. An imposing figure in flowing *agbad*a and traditional Yoruba *fila* cap[1]. Now he looked in dismay at the big dent in his magnificent car.

"Who did this? Who smashed into my car," he demanded. I quickly stepped in. I explained who I was and that the Prince was my driver and it was he who had slammed into his car. We were, I added, planning to return to Lagos before nightfall.

"So," said the big man, "you're the director of the NIJ. He smiled and relaxed a bit. "I know Lateef Jakande well. I'll fix things up with him. And you, he added, jabbing a long finger at the Prince, "you will come with me to the police station. Let us see if you can walk a straight line. Somehow I don't think you can."

A couple of hours later they returned from the police station. The Prince had failed the straight line challenge and a few other tests as well. I cannot recall whether he had been charged, but he was back and still keen to drive.

I advise you strongly not to let him drive, even after a sleep," said the big man.

We needed no urging. I took over the driving and drove to the interstate bus terminus. Someone else could enjoy the Prince's company. Before stepping into the Lagos-bound bus, he paused to roundly curse us. And he didn't stop there. He cursed our parents. He cursed our ancestors. He was still cursing as the passengers, impatient to get going, cajoled him.

"Come on old man," they taunted, "get inside the bus. We can't wait all day."

By this time, his gunny sack of bush rats was quite on the nose, the folly of tying them to a red hot manifold.

So, with me at the wheel and Diana navigating, we set off for home, with high hopes of making it in daylight. Our journey by necessity was slowed by the shocking condition of the road. We had to negotiate huge potholes, some as big as mini craters.

It was like a moonscape, a legacy of the neglect that followed the Biafra war. Jagged, sharp edges on the highway added to the danger. Evidence of the disastrous civil war was clearly visible in the east, not only in the state of the roads, but in the tell-tale marks of bullet-scarred buildings.

More than one million people died in the war that raged from July 1966 to 1970 and was ultimately won by the Federal forces against the breakaway Biafran state of which the Igbo were the dominant ethnic group.

The military government did its best to paper over the lingering wounds of the conflict by adopting an even-handed approach in shuffling the tribal composition of its departments between the three main ethic groups — Hausa (from the north), Yoruba (from the west and south) and Igbo from the east. Thus one government department might be headed, say, by a Hausa, with a Yoruba as deputy. Another would have a Yoruba in charge, and maybe an Igbo as deputy. And so on until all three ethnic groups were in some sort of balance.

Commerce was encouraged between the former warring states. Merchants from the republican side, for example, would set up shop in the former Biafra.

But divisions and distrust ran deep. No obstacles were put in the path of Yorubas and Hausas setting up stores, but, our sources told us, few would buy their produce. So, in small measure, it was case of Biafran pay-back.

Back on the road, we were making slow but steady progress. And we felt safer now that the Prince and his rats and yams were no longer with us. Then CLUNK. The car hit a rough patch and we limped lamely along until we at last came to a service station. I can't recall what part of the car was damaged, but it was bad enough to lay us up for an hour or two while repairs were made.

We were worried now. We had lost valuable time and it was vital that we made Lagos before dark. Not only because of the state of the road and the traffic weaving side to side trying to avoid the potholes, but because of the threat of highway robbers.

Their favourite ruse was to chop down a large tree so that it fell across the road. A motorist coming on to the scene would naturally think it was simply the result of wind damage and consider his options: do I go off the road and skirt around the blockage. Or do I turn around and seek another route? While the driver hesitated, the armed robbers would rush out from their bush cover and demand money or car. Maybe both. Refusal could offend. Fatally.

Some years later in Kenya, we were told of an incident that made the hair on our necks stand up. We had thrown a party for our friends, including our Kenyan newspaper colleagues and among them was this long-term English resident At about 10 o'clock, when the party was just getting warmed up, he took me aside, said he had had a good time, but now had to leave.

"Why so early?" I asked. "We haven't even had supper yet. Are you feeling unwell or something."

"No, sorry, he replied apologetically, "it's just that it is unsafe if I don't get home before 11 o'clock."

"Why on earth is it unsafe?"

"Because that is when the armed robbers come out to set up ambushes for motorists." Realising a fuller explanation was called for he told me this story:

"I was driving home one night after a party. It was around eleven, maybe a bit later, when I came to a spot where a tree had fallen across the road. My path was completely blocked. I looked at the tree. It was not overly large and I thought my VW Beetle would not have too much trouble getting over it. So I started to do just that — drive over it.

"But the Beetle was making hard work of it. I then had the weird sensation that the car was leaving the ground. I looked out the window and saw why: ropes had been tied to each side of the tree and the car was becoming airborne.

"Then I saw them. About eight or nine thugs were hauling furiously on the ropes. Christ. I began to panic. I revved up the Beetle, but it seemed to be stuck on the trunk of the tree.

"I couldn't go forward, so in desperation I gunned the car in reverse. It gave an almighty shudder and dropped back onto the road. I did a hasty U-turn, put my foot down on the accelerator and got the hell out of there. As I did so the bandits swarmed out of the bush, banging on the doors with clubs, cutlasses and pelting the car with rocks.

"You can see why I now go home early from parties."

No such misadventure befell us in Nigeria, but our nerves were nevertheless on edge as we sped along the highway towards Lagos. Despite our concern, we reached the outskirts of Lagos just on dusk.

A day or two later, I was seated at my desk in the office, when in strolled the Prince. As if nothing had happened. What gall. I looked directly at him and said: "Prince, you are fired."

He just shrugged and walked out. What happened to his yams and bush rats I wouldn't know. But the rats, as well as the Prince, must have been truly on the nose.

Several years later in Nairobi, on the other side of Africa, we heard of a teacher who fell victim to an embarrassing carjack crime. The teacher was driving a few kilometres out of town, when bandits forced him at gunpoint to stop and hand over the keys to his SUV and his money.

But they didn't stop there, taking his clothes after stripping him all the way down to his jocks. He was walking along the side of the road when a man he knew recognised him and drove him home.

It was a time when four-wheel drive vehicles, such as Pajeros, were becoming the flavour of the month for carjackers. And you did not argue with them. Even walking home almost nude was better than the alternative.

Chapter 10

HANDSHAKE FEAR GRIPS IMO STATE

This was the clever and quirky headline that appeared in one of the country's newspapers during our stay. Its genesis was in the belief that if you shook hands with a stranger (superstition suggested it was a warlock) your male genitals would drop off. Or at least wither on the vine. In 1979 the outbreak of handshake fear reached endemic proportion in some states, particularly in the south-eastern state of Imo.

Complaints flooded in from the countryside of men meeting strangers, shaking hands with them and, with a gasp, reaching down to "discover" that their genitals had vanished. *Don quenched,* as they put it pidgin.

The fever spread to other states. The *Lagos Weekend* cashed in on the phenomenon in June 1979 under the compelling all-caps headline OPERATION PULL YOUR PANTS. The story read:

Handshake fear grips Imoh State

"It was a real show at the police station in Auchi, Bendel State, recently when several men came in to exhibit their male organs.

"There were long ones and the short ones, but the owners alleged they were altogether useless.

"Why?

"They were alleged to have fallen victim of "mysterious" men who paraded the town. Recently, rumours spread like wild fire that some people lost their organs as a result of their shaking hands with the "mysterious men". Since the rumour there have been several unsavoury scenes on Auchi streets. Many people had escaped being lynched only by a hair's breadth.

"On one occasion, a housewife received a bullet wound by the police to save her from the hands of those who suspected her to have caused the loss of his male organ.

"On June 1, four men, including a teacher at Otaru Grammar School, Auchi, reported they were victims of a "shake hands and lose your organ" incident.

"Rumours of these incidents had since spread into other areas of the Etsako Local Governments areas — towns like Owen, Okpedho and Agbazilo."

And then the punch line:

"However, a medical consultant at the Auchi General Hospital, Dr E.M. Akinluyi, dismissed the rumours as false.

"This ugly rumour cannot be substantiated by the so-called victims as each of the eight persons physically examined had his male organ intact and erect," he told *Times* man Sam Dimawoh recently."

But back to Imo State where it all began. Things looked pretty desperate until the Governor, or some important person, came up with a brilliant strategy. Exquisite in its simplicity. First he commandeered a tray-top truck, in which he positioned two strong, athletic looking and stark-naked police constables. Then he installed a strongly amplified public address system in the cabin. As the truck moved slowly through the crowds, the smiling policemen vigorously shook hands.

"See, they do not drop off," said the man behind the PA microphone. "Shake hands with your brother. Shake hands with your mother. Shake hands with a friend. Shake hands with a stranger. They do not drop off. I repeat they do not drop off."

Writing for *Encyclopaedia Britannica,* Ibo Cbanga says juju, a form of witchcraft, is practised in West African countries such as Nigeria, Benin, Togo and Ghana. It is neither good nor bad, but can be used for constructive purposes as well as nefarious deeds. Cbanga says a monkey's head is the most common juju and that juju operates on the principle of spiritual contagious contact based on physical contact. Thus, it is possible to manipulate one in order to reach the other.

A person's hair, fingernails, a piece of clothing, a shoe, a sock, or an item of jewellery are "are all candidates for juju because they are believed to retain the spiritual aura of the owner". In other words Charms and mascots, as the writer points out, are all common forms of juju and are worn to protect against ill fortune and evil spirits.

Cbanga adds: "Specialists with expensive know-how and experience typically create juju. The specialist may be a healer, because juju is commonly used as treatment for physical and spiritual ailments — from healing insect and animal bites to counteracting and neutralising curses.

"However, the specialist may also be a witch or sorcerer trying to harm someone through the casting of spells or curses, as well as placing juju objects in their close contact so they may become spiritually contaminated and polluted. For instance, one may be offered spiritually poisoned food or drinks, which is thought to bring about disruption, trauma, or even death if not dealt with promptly and efficiently.

A live animal may also be used as a juju. It may be infused with a negative energy and then sent near someone. Once physical contact has been made, it is believed the person will most likely become ill."

This goes a long way to explain how in the 1970s phenomena like "handshake fear" and operation "pull your pants" can enter the realm of believability. So when a victim of juju magic says he has lost his genitals, the conviction in his mind becomes, to him, reality.

At the Institute, there was gossip that one of the lecturers possessed a juju stone which he kept in his pocket and used it to traumatise a fellow teacher.

Chapter 11

REBELS AND WRITERS

Nigeria has always had a bad press abroad and, for many reasons, justly so. In the 1970s there was no Boko Haram or similar terror groups. However, there was widespread corruption and violent crime — and violent punishment — as well as extreme poverty. There was oil aplenty, but the wealth it provided never got through to the people and oil spills despoiled the land.

Educated Nigerians were highly critical of the many wrongs in society, but bristled when outsiders joined in the chorus of condemnation. Michael Olumide, the charismatic former head of the Nigerian Broadcasting Corporation, once told me: "There is a lot wrong with Nigeria, but when outsiders try to tell us what's wrong with us, I jump to the country's defence."

In fact there is also much to admire in Nigeria — certainly not in its history of corrupt and unstable government, but in the richness of its culture, the resilience of its people and the courage of its robust press. The nation has produced writers of outstanding quality. Some, such as Chinua Achebe, Wole Soyinka and Tai Solarin have international reputations.

Others of note include Chimand Ngozi Adichie, Ben Okri and Cyprian Ekweni. Chinua Achebe's novel *Things Fall Apart* — the story of a tribesman forced into exile and later to suicide — has sold well over one million copies. It was his first of several novels. The book, first published in 1958, was prescribed reading for the Institute's English class during our time in Nigeria.

Wole Soyinka, now in his 80s, was an outstanding political activist, educator, playwright and novelist. His output was prolific, with publication of hundreds of works. The pinnacle of success came in 1986 when he was awarded the Nobel Prize for Literature. In his acceptance speech, Soyinka dedicated the award to Nelson Mandela.

Whipping up controversy and giving the authorities a hard time during our stay in the country, was another rebel with a cause called Tai Solarin. Described by the British newspaper *The Independent* as a national icon, Solarin, primarily an educator, was a fierce social critic and adversary of the military government of the day. He used shock tactics with spectacular success, notably in the way he drew attention to the way bodies were often left to rot in the streets of Lagos and Ibadan, a teeming city of millions, 118 kilometres north of the capital.

There was good reason for this disregard for human life as so much animal road kill. From time to time, we were told, good Samaritans had reported the presence of bodies, presumably the victims of hit-run drivers or some other misadventure, to the police. Big mistake. When they eventually turned up, the police often detained the good Samaritans on suspicion of involvement in the deaths.

Understandably, the good Samaritans withdrew from the scene. Enter Tai Solarin. Utterly fed up with the failure of his ministrations to the authorities to collect and respect the dead from the streets, Solarin took matters into his own hands. He collected a body from an Ibadan street, put it in a coffin and delivered to the steps of City Hall. It stayed there for several days.

Every now and then, an individual from the health department would emerge, give the coffin a few whiffs of deodorant from an aerosol can and scuttle back into his office. This farce went on for some time, until the smell of death became so overpowering that the authorities did what they should have done in the first place — removed and disposed of the body. Hopefully, they did it in a dignified manner.

All these great men of culture were bound by a common theme: a rebellious streak that displayed contempt for official sloth, corruption and hypocrisy. And they harried, harassed and ridiculed with flair.

Making huge headlines in 1977 was a first cousin of Wole Soyinka's called Olufela Anikulapo-Kuti. Or just plain Fela to his many thousands of fans. Fela was a sensation, an extraordinarily gifted talent, famous for his unique Afrobeat music[1], his merciless baiting of the military government and his sexual appetites.

Fela was a national legend, a singer-songwriter who could play the saxophone, keyboards, drums, trumpet and guitar. He came from the highly talented Ransome-Kuti family described by Britain's *Guardian* newspaper as "the Kennedys of Nigeria".[1]

His mother was a renowned feminist during colonial times, his father an Anglican priest and leading educator and his two brothers were doctors. Fela dropped the "Ransome" from his name and replaced it with "Anikulapo". The new name means "he who carries death in his pouch" which, as things turned out, had an eerily prophetic ring to it. The fuse that ignited a disastrous chain of events was lit in 1977 — our first year in Nigeria — when Fela and his Afrika '70 band released their smash hit Zombie,[2] a scathing attack on the military and the way its soldiers, zombie-like, mutely followed orders. The first verse sets the scene.

Zombie o Zombie (Zombie o Zombie) x 2
Zombie no go unless you tell am to go
(Zombie)
Zombie no go stop unless you tell am to stop
(Zombie)
Zombie no go turn unless you tell am to turn
(Zombie)
Zombie no go think unless you tell am to think
(Zombie)
Zombie o Zombie
Zombie o Zombie

The taunts were taken up by people in the street and were chanted whenever they had an urge to insult the army or police.

The military were incandescent with rage. The soldiers raided the Shrine, Fela's commune, HQ and nightclub not once, but twice. Fela was badly beaten and his 75-year-old mother, Fumilayo, thrown out of a first floor window, dying the following year from her injuries. The Shrine was burnt to the ground. (4) Another Zombie verse, in Pidgin English and Yoruba (Fela's mother tongue) goes:

Go and kill (joro jara joro)
go and die (joro jara joro)
go and quench (joro jara joro)
put am in reverse (joro jara joro)
go and quench (joro jara joro)
go and kill (joro jara joro)
go and die (joro jara joro)
put am for reverse (jaro and jara joro)

And finally, the last verse which again stresses the blind zombie-like unquestioning of orders:

attention! (zombie)
quick march (zombie)
slow march (zombie)
right turn (zombie)
about turn (zombie)
double up (zombie)
salute (zombie)

In February 1978 Fela, in an extraordinary gesture of compassion and macho manhood, married twenty-seven of his female entourage, many of them dancers and members of his chorus. Some of them had also been beaten in the raids. He called them his queens and claimed to have made love to all of them. Later he divorced them on the grounds that marriage was selfish and created jealousy.

Diana and I never got to meet Fela, but we did see him in action. It so happened that our dentist, Fran, was Fela's niece and Fran was about to get married. Who else but Fela and Afrika '70 would entertain? We were duly invited to take our place among the lucky guests.

On the big night, a stage was constructed on a large platform truck parked in the street outside Fran's house. Fela, stripped to his waist, sweat dripping off his body, played and sang his heart out before the scores of guests. His energy was amazing. For sheer magnetic appeal he reminded me of a sort of black Mick Jagger.

Fela and his band were really hitting their straps when, out of the blue, NEPA pulled the plug. To cries of "Nepa don quench", the lights went out and the band stopped playing. But it wasn't a premature ending. Someone, presumably, paid the bribe and, after an enforced intermission, the lights came on and to wild cheers the show went on.

I cannot recall whether Fela and the Afrika '70 played the Zombie hit. I fancy not, because it would have been unforgettable. Fela died in August 1997 from complications caused by AIDS. He was 58.

Chapter 12

MISTER COOL

The Press in Nigeria has always had a rough and ready image: the prose has lacked form and syntax and the abundance of schoolboy howlers has provided endless entertainment for its expatriate critics. The design and layout as often been untidy and lacking clarity. But its Press has never lacked courage.

Its journalists have always been fearless and gutsy — even during periods of colonial and military rule. They have gone to jail for their beliefs and principles and emerged as strong and feisty as ever.

Just as the country has spawned famous activists, writers and poets, so too has it given birth to many fine, brave and talented journalists. My boss at the Nigerian Institute of Journalism, Alhaji Lateef Jakande, chairman of the Board of Governors, was among the best. In earlier days, Jakande was a forthright columnist with the *Nigerian Tribune*, writing under *the nom de plume* of John West. Chief Dayo Duyile in his voluminous tome, *Makers of Nigerian Press*, pays this tribute to Jakande:

"John West was ruthless in his handlings of any national issue. Like The *Tribune*, John West had the stamina to survive all odds. So influential, so incisive, were John West columns that the former Prime Minister, Sir Abubaker Tafewa Balewa, remarked: 'If I had my way, I would tuck away this John West.' The Prime Minister's wish was caused, presumably, by Lateef Jakande's columns always playing the Peeping Tom'."

Jakande, born in 1929, always had his eye on the political stage, and in 1979 at the end of my stay, he became the first civilian Governor of Lagos State. From 1992 to 1998, he was Minister of works in Sani Abacha's military government. In this role, he established the Lagos State University. His many reforms included providing low-cost housing for the poor. After the military coup of 1983, Jakande's crusading spirit took a severe setback when he fell foul of the government and was charged and convicted of treason. He was later pardoned when democracy was restored in 1999.

Jakande was one of the coolest operators I have met. I never saw him rattled and I never saw him lose his temper or raise his voice. He had a calm authority, but there was never any doubt as to who was in command.

He also had a good sense of humour. On one occasion, frustrated with the delay it took to get answers from a certain quarter, I remarked: "Some people have a very elastic sense of time." Jakande chuckled. The expression tickled him pink.

In his talks to groups of young journalists, I recall him giving this advice:

"When you go to functions, you will often be offered alcohol. My advice is you may drink, but don't get drunk. As a reporter you need a clear head and you can't get that if you drink too much."

One of my duties as Director of the Institute was to organise seminars, to which, depending on the topic, I would invite leaders in business, industry, agriculture and education to be the keynote speaker. The oil industry seminar, for example, was an important one and always got good media coverage.

Frankly, the seminars were begging bowls, albeit sophisticated ones, when Jakande would use all his persuasive skills of oratory in asking the captains of industry to dig deep and support the cause of journalism, that is, the Nigerian Institute of Journalism.

It was fascinating to watch the Chairman speak. He always spoke without notes — an expert of the off-the-cuff variety. He used no props, but at lunch-time at a seminar he would pick up and twiddle a spoon or fork as he spoke. My theory about time and elasticity was put to the test at the convocation of 1978. Traditionally, the Chairman would make a speech and then the Director would hand the diplomas to him for presentation to the graduands. On this night, the hall was packed with parents, relative, teachers and eager-faced students patiently awaiting the appearance of Alhaji Jakande.

Time ticked by. No appearance. Time stretched to well after the appointed time. No Jakande. The audience was becoming restless. Finally, I decided to deliver my own speech, hoping I would not have to present the diplomas. My prepared speech was relatively short, but I eked it out. Each word was enunciated with measured care.

I stressed every syllable and paused after every sentence. Then, finally ending the speechmaker's equivalent of the slow march, I bit the bullet and started to present the diplomas.

Like magic, this was the undeclared signal for the Chairman to make his entrance. To thunderous applause he strolled unhurriedly up the aisle and onto the dais. Then with customary charisma and aplomb took over the show.

By now, Jakande was well into planning his foray into politics. Around at the *Tribune* office, his waiting room was always full of fellow countrymen, calmly awaiting an audience to press their views and aims. Some had been waiting hours. Jakande would work extraordinary hours, often late into the night. His only concession was to have a half-hour catnap before resuming as before.

Towards the end of my contract, the Chairman sprang a huge surprise on me. "I would like you to draw up a design for the new NIJ headquarters at Ikeja," he said casually. IKeja, on the Lagos mainland, was to be the final home for the Institute, replacing the ramshackle wooden building in Breadfruit Street. I could hardly believe my ears. When I had recovered from the shock, I stammered something like: "Mr Chairman, about the only thing I can draw is a salary. Surely this is a task for an architect."

"No," said Jakande, "I want you to do it. The general concept. How it will look. The architect can attend to the technical drawings."

So design it I did. I sketched a large rectangle. In the centre was a big auditorium-cum-assembly hall. Around the hall I allowed for offices, library, toilet block and some classrooms. Upstairs were more classrooms and provision for limited living quarters. It was very basic, but served the purpose.

Of course, it cried out for professional input — which it eventually received — but at least it was a big step up from my classroom doodling days.

Some years later I returned, with the Canadian journalist Murray Burt to teach a short course in design and sub-editing to candidates from the nation's newspapers. To my surprise, the course was held in the new NIJ building at Ikeja on the mainland. And to my even greater surprise it looked just as I had envisaged. With the addition of a soccer pitch!

Actually, Jakande was over-generous when, in a farewell letter of appreciation, he wrote (in part):

"Your contribution has been very significant. Not only did you improve on the content of the courses offered by the Institute, you added the considerable administrative job of seeing through the long-standing project of constructing the new 1.4 million naira headquarters of the Nigerian Institute of Journalism. You also overcame a number of student crises with admirable courage and a keen sense of humour which has always impressed me."

Jakande became editor-in-chief of *The Tribun*e in 1956 and much later founded John West Publications to publish *The Lagos News*. He was heavily involved in the International Press Institute, which set up the NIJ and was President of the Newspaper Publishers Association of Nigeria.

Chapter 13

SHEER GUTS

The popular press showed its courage when, in the mid-1970s, *Nigerian Observer* journalist Minere Amakiri had the audacity to upset the military Governor of Rivers State, Diette Spiff, on his birthday. His crime? Reporting the mass resignation of teachers.

Retribution was swift and merciless. Amakiri was thrown into prison and his head shaved with a rusty razor blade. Some sources said it was with a broken bottle. The National Press ran a relentess campaign to have the reporter freed. One newspaper years later was still running the rallying call **REMEMBER AMAKIRI** under its masthead. The campaign won the day and Amakiri was later awarded damages. The brutality of the military regime did not harm his future prospects and he became publisher and editor-in-chief of *The Beacon* newspaper. Amakiri died in 2011.

Worse was to come in 1986 under the Government of General Ibrahim Babangida. A new quality magazine called *Newswatch* was setting new standards in investigative journalism. Its founders were Dan Agbese, Dele Giwa, Ray Ekpu and Yakubu Mohammed. Its team was fearless. But its truth-at-all-cost approach led to fateful results. On 19 October, 1986, Dele Giwa was relaxing at his home in Ikeja. He was about to eat a meal with Kayode Soyinka, the *Newswatch* London bureau chief, when a large brown parcel addressed to him was delivered by two men in a Peugeot car.

The parcel carried what appeared to be the official Government seal. Dele believed it had come from the office of President General Babangida. When he attempted to open it, the parcel blew up, almost severing the lower half of his body.

It was the first Nigerian assassination of a journalist. Two days before Dele had been interrogated by a security agent who falsely accused him of gun-running and planning to destabilise the Government.

In 1987 *Newswatch* was banned for six months by the Babangida regime for allegedly violating the Official Secrets Act. The offence: running stories revealing the recommendations of a Presidential commission devising a new political system.

Ray Ekpu, who was a colleague of mine on the committee of the Commonwealth Journalists Association, continued to promote, with distinction, freedom of the press. He presided over the CJA at its conferences in Hong Kong in 1997 (the year of the return of the colony to China) and Windhoek in 1994.

Chapter 14

ASSASSINATION

In 1979, about half way through our final year, it became apparent that Diana was pregnant. Her distinguished gynaecologist was Norman Williams, an African who owed the anglicised version of his name to descendants from the old slave days. Confirming that Diana was indeed pregnant, Norman Williams instructed her to provide a specimen.

"But don't take it to my surgery," he said."I visit the Polo Club every Monday, so take it there and tell the barman to store it safely until I arrive." Diana did just that: labelled the jar with name, date and other details and secured it in a brown paper bag. Then she rocked up at the male-dominated club and handed it to the head barman with the instructions that it would be picked up by Williams on his next visit.

Taking custody of the specimen, the curious barman could not resist taking the jar out of the bag for closer inspection before stowing it in the fridge. Diana's face blushed crimson as dozens of Polo Club drinkers craned necks to see what the magic potion was that this white woman had brought to the club.

Pretty risky, I thought. What would happen if the barman making the dry martinis absentmindedly mixed up the wrong ingredients?

All went well of course. Norman Williams safely executed the pick-up and tests confirmed the pregnancy. He looked after his patient well, visiting her at home instead of the surgery and gave her special instructions:

"In an emergency," he told her, "you must ring me." Then, he added:

"I have four phones.

"The one at the surgery doesn't work.

"The one at my rooms at the hospital occasionally works.

"The one at my home never works, nor does the one at my city office."

"So how CAN I get in touch?" asked Diana anxiously."

"Ring the Chief Justice. He has a phone.

"And it works."

So, in a way, that was the beginning of Imogen Roberts Lawrence: Conceived in Nigeria, learned to walk and talk in China, educated in Kenya and Australia and wed in Bali. Truly an international child.

There was a humorous post-script to this story. Shortly before we left for home, I was interviewed by *The Punch*, a lively daily newspaper. After chatting about my work, the future of the media, what I thought of the Nigerian press and related themes, I rounded off with the words:

"After all, my wife is having a Nigerian baby." Which caused some confusion and a few chuckles — at least until Imogen was born.

Our first adventure in "deepest, darkest Africa" was coming to an end. After nearly two years we flew out on a meandering trip home, dropping off for visits to England, Italy, India and Singapore. By this time Diana was largely pregnant, almost fulfilling, at least in part, the Immigration officer's invitation to "have many babies here".

Our exit was markedly different to our entrance when we came in through the old hot-as-hell airport. In its place was a shiny brand-new facility, named after the assassinated Head of State, General Murtala Muhammed. Muhammed had come to power on 29 July 1975 after a military coup, one of seven in Nigeria's chequered history as it struggled with the concept of democracy.

The general was ambushed in a classic Lagos go-slow, the traffic jams that frequently paralysed the capital, and died in a hail of bullets fired by Lieutenant-Colonel Buka Suka Dimka and his fellow army plotters.

It was 13 February 1976 and Muhammed and his aide de camp, Lieut-general Akitunde Akinsehinwa, were returning to Dodan Barracks when their car was halted by the go-slow. It was the perfect ambush. Dimka, and a handful of rebel soldiers strolled up to the black Mercedes and riddled the car and its occupants with rapid fire.

Dimka, according to my sources, then escaped, calmly strolling through the maze of cars and people, casually shaking hands with some of them. According to some reports, he then went to the NBC Radio studios and bragged over the airwaves that the coup had succeeded. It had not.

After melting into the population, Colonel Dimka checked

into a hotel, posing as a Mr C. Godwin of the Federal Ministry of Education. The military, tipped off, closed in but Dimka escaped yet again, bolting through a toilet window.

His pursuers finally caught up with him at a checkpoint on 5 March 1976 and on 15 May, along with seven other conspirators, he was executed by firing squad after being found guilty of treason and murder. The pictures of the executions were published in gory detail by the *Unilag Sun*, journal of the University of Lagos.

Muhammad was just 37. The black Mercedes staff car has a special spot at the National Museum. Diana and I paid a special visit to the museum and saw how bullets had peppered holes in doors, windows and windscreens. The display chillingly captured the moment of death. Muhammed never had a chance.

During our stay, the Military Government of Olusegun Obasanjo decided there had simply been too many coups and attempted coups. So it promulgated an edict, published under this headline in a daily newspaper:

COUPS OUTLAWED

The irony of a government that came to power in a coup, now claiming the moral high ground, was just too exquisite.

Chapter 15

A NEW CRISIS

Just as our arrival at the old airport had begun with a crisis, so did our exit at the new terminal. I had just cleared immigration and was heading for the departure lounge when I turned around to beckon Diana on. I was alarmed to glimpse her just as she disappeared into a booth, escorted by a female security officer.

It was one of those annoying random body searches common at most international airports. As the minutes ticked by my anxiety grew. After perhaps a half hour Diana emerged ashen-faced from the booth.

She recounted what happened. As the security officer patted her down she paused and said:

"What is this?"

"What is what?" said Diana.

"This!" said the woman prodding Diana firmly in the chest.

"Oh that. It's just my bra."

"No, what is that! What are you hiding in your bra?" said the officer with an aggressive edge to her voice. Diana felt a sudden surge of panic. Her grandmother, in a farewell gesture, had slipped a $50 note into her hand. Diana had forgotten all about the gift until later, when she was packing to go home. The money had not been declared on entry, so she slipped into her bra.

Wrong move.

"It's just a few dollars my grandma gave as a farewell present," my wife told the searcher.

"Where is your declaration that you brought this money into the country?"

"I didn't make one. Look I am terribly, terribly sorry, I just forgot," said Diana fighting back tears. "It's not a lot of money."

"It is illegal to bring undeclared foreign currency into Nigeria," said the security officer.

"Please, I'm truly sorry. My husband will be frantic and our plane is about to leave."

There was an ominous silence. For a minute Diana felt she was going to be detained. Then the officer relented.

"Go! Go!" she shouted. "Next time obey the law."

Diana didn't need a second invitation and scuttled off to join me in the departure lounge. We boarded the aircraft and, hearts beating rapidly, took our seats, expected any second to hear the dreaded Call: "Will Mr and Mrs Lawrence please leave the aircraft and report to the desk."

The call never came. Under my breath I prayed: "Please God, if we crash, don't let us crash in Nigeria." It was almost a classic case of Murphy's Law one and two. What can go wrong, will go wrong and what will go wrong will go wrong at the worst possible time.

Part Two

Chapter 16

BACK TO AFRICA

Eight years later, in 1986, we were back in Africa, following two long assignments in China where I helped set up *China Daily*, the first English daily newspaper in the People's Republic. But that's another story. This time it was Kenya, described by the popular South African novelist Wilbur Smith as a microcosm of Africa: Savannah, jungle, desert, tropical beaches and a snow-clad mountain, the 3,825-metre Mt Kenya.

Actually once there were two snow-clad mountains, until the western colonial powers of Britain, France and Germany in typical colonial arrogance, tweeked the boundaries and gave the majestic 5,895-metre Mt Kilimanjaro to German-controlled Tanganyika (now Tanzania following the 1964 merger with the spice island of Zanzibar).[1]

Our destination was Nairobi, a capital city of about 1,700,000 people when we arrived and today a sprawling metropolis of 3.5 million. The name comes from the Maasai words *Enkare Nyrobi*[2] which means *cold water.* I had been granted two years leave of absence from *The Age* newspaper in Melbourne to take up the post of Training Editor with the Aga Khan's *Daily Nation* group of newspapers. I stayed nearly nine years until my abrupt departure.

After the day-by-day battle for survival in Lagos, Nairobi was a welcome relief. We lived in a modest, but comfortable bungalow-style house built on a half-acre of land, in the leafy suburb of Kileleshwa. The property was close to a well-treed but neglected arboretum from which vervet moneys would sometimes visit us and taunt our dogs from the lower branches of trees along our boundary fence. The bird life was prolific. Squirrels scurried around in the bushes and there were mongooses which created havoc when they invaded our chicken coop and decimated the inhabitants — a cute clutch of *kuku kidogo* (bantam chooks).

We inherited a Kamba *shamba man* (gardener) called Peter and took on a Kikuyu house-keeper called Florence, eschewing the usual epithet of *"house girl"*. Although the Kikuyu and Kamba were related tribes, Florence and Peter enjoyed, at best, an uneasy truce.

You never did for yourself in Kenya. As soon as you moved into new digs, the bush telegraph went into high alert. Dozens of job-seekers would come rattling the gates looking for jobs as house-keepers, child-minders, cooks and gardeners. In the Kenyan economy of the time these were relatively well-paid positions.

Florence had had previous experience with expat families and liked to pick up food recipe hints. Like her specialty chocolate cake. It was simply delicious and survives in our card recipe index to this day. Some of the western culinary habits intrigued her, like the night we had lobster for dinner. Florence had never seen lobster — after all, it's not the sort of delicacy that you we see on the average Kenyan dinner table — and after we had polished it off she approached Diana with a request: "Could I have the skin please madam?"

"Yes, "replied Diana, "but why on earth would you want a useless shell?"

"I want to scare my friends. I am going to nail it above my doorway. They are going to get a big fright."

Strange.

We could only put it down to some sort of superstition. Or ju ju. It was not like Florence. Did the lobster skin scare her friends, we later asked. Like a treat said Florence. It was a great practical joke. Florence knew quite a bit about food as her husband, Johnson, was a chef with a schools catering firm. When we learned that his *piece de resistance* was samosas we asked Florence if we could pay Johnson to make some for us. Just the thing to serve at a curry party or at a barbecue.

Yes, he could, said Florence and six dozen meat and vegetable samosas made their way into our freezer. They were just about the best samosas we had ever had — or at least on a par with those our Indian friends made. Years later, we are still trying to find samosas to equal them in Australia.

Florence and Johnson, like so many other so-called servants, had a small farm in Kiambu. Peter also had a farm in Kamba territory and one day approached me with sad news. "My bull," he bemoaned, "she is dead."

"Sorry to hear that Peter," I replied, adroitly ignoring the subtle hint that I should pay for a replacement bull.

From time to time we gave cuts of meat — legs of lamb or pieces of beef — to Florence, who also had to provide for her young son Charles who lived with her in the two rooms, provided by *Nation*, separated from the main house. Of course, other expats often gave food to their domestic staff.

Some, still living the colonial life, were not so forthcoming, giving inferior cuts known as "staff meat" to their domestic staff. Or, to their everlasting shame, some would ask their butcher for "head meat". These were the people who would refer to personal staff as "house boy" or "house girl. Terms that had not only a tinge or racism, but were semantically absurd considering a so-called house boy could well be a man in his 50s or 60s.

Florence, like so many Kenyan women at the time had a pressing problem: how to stop having so many children. Or, in her case, how to refuse without giving offence to Johnson's demands for sex. Again, like so many Kenyan women, Florence most probably did not practise birth control. The answer when it came was akin to a miracle. A chance remark from Diana about the internationally acclaimed Marie Stopes fertility clinic set Florence's mind racing.

Questions flew: how did they do it? How *did* they tie the tubes? Did the procedure leave any scars? What was the success rate? Were there any health risks?

Then came the BIG decision. "Madam," said Florence one day, "I want to do it. I want to have this operation."

"Florence, that's great news. I'll make an appointment and take you there."

Unlike many Kenyan husbands, who were opposed to birth control, Johnson readily gave permission for the procedure to go ahead. And so Florence had her tubes tied. The keyhole surgery at the Nairobi clinic amazed Florence. "There's just a tiny hole in my tummy," she confided to Diana. Amazing."

To put Florence's experience in context, we need to point out that the fertility rate (the number of births per woman) when we first arrived in Kenya, was about eight. By 2016, according to World Bank statistics, it had fallen to 3.9.

This is a huge drop in the fertility rate and is due to increasing educational levels and a greater acceptance of contraceptive methods. Back in the 1980s there was an attitude of God will take care of me, aided and abetted by the narrow approach of the church to birth control. It was an attitude I struck sometimes in discussions in the *Nation* newsroom.

Back in Australia one year on holidays, I was taken aback to be asked at a party: “Do you have slaves in your house in Africa?” It was a new year party and little too much of the good stuff, I opine, must have gone to my interlocutor’s head.

Strange, as it may sound, the domestic staff who worked for ex-pats in our time, formed part of the Kenyan middle class. You had only had to observe what happened when word got around that a family was leaving. The bush telegraph got cracking and in no time and *wananchi* would be clamouring at the front gate looking for a job.

Working for ex-pats was a highly prized occupation. However, it was a stratified system. Americans paid the most, leading to some whinging that the Yanks were spoiling it for everyone. Generally, we were told, African domestics preferred working for Western ex-pats, followed by Indians and last of all came Africans working for Africans. During our Nigerian days, Ben Opolo, one of the Institute’s lecturers, had a girl working in his house and she must have been no older than nine or ten, and most probably a relative.

*

Nairobi is 1,795 metres (about 4,500 feet) above sea level and extremes of weather are rare. The mercury seldom rises above 32 degrees Celsius and at night it is a typical 14 degrees. So you can sleep comfortably with maybe one light blanket on the bed.

Thus we got, for the most part, an almost perfect climate — a cross between the temperate and the tropical. In our *shamba* we could grow paw paws, bananas and chokoes. While at a nearby friend's place, a small tree simply sagged and split under the weight of mangos.

Yet we could easily grow green beans and we had a show bed of English roses: Just Joey, Ice ginger and Princess Elizabeth. Kenya, in fact, is famous for its horticulture, and in the Lake Naivasha region, beans — straight as an arrow, not a bend in sight — and other fresh vegetables are exported to Europe daily by special freight aircraft.

We had two wet seasons — the short rains which fall for a few weeks in November and December — and the long rains in March, April and May when the days become gloomy and low cloud cover hangs around for days. Old-timers and expatriates referred to the oppressive build-up to the long rains as suicide month.

Despite the mild to warm weather, the climate changes dramatically a few score kilometres south-west from the capital on the way to Lake Magadi. You quickly find yourself in a dry hot environment as the road spirals down rapidly in tight twists and turns for 112 kilometres. You are now at the lowest point of the Rift Valley in East Africa and just 600 metres above sea level.

It is a drive that calls for caution, not only for the steepness of the road, but because of the wildlife that can suddenly jump out in front of a vehicle. An acquaintance broke both legs after his four-wheel drive collided with a giraffe.

Magadi is a hot soda lake and the soda is harvested and sold as soda ash. The Lake attracts hundreds of flamingos, which pick their way through the shallow water, filtering their food — brine shrimp and planktonic bloom — through their purpose-built bills. It is this diet that gives the naturally grey flamingos their spectacular pink plumage. You also see flamingos in great number at Lakes Nakuru, Bogoria and Elementeita.

Chapter 17

A DOG'S LIFE

Security was tight in Kenya and, like everyone else, we had bars on our windows and a portcullis separated the rest of the house from the main bedroom. However, despite the security, our attitude was relaxed. You were safe if you took prudent precautions: An *askari* (sentry) patrolled the property and we had dogs. Most people, expats and citizens alike, had this sign outside their homes:

Mbwa Kali

Which translates to Fierce Dog.

We had two *shenzi* (mixed breed) dogs, Grotty and Brin, and two mini dachshunds, Zoe and Cleo, which, along with two giant tortoises, Jessica and Annabel, completed our Kenya family.

Grotty was a great dog, rescued from a river after being dumped there in a bag to drown. He was in an emaciated condition when the Kenya Society for the Prevention of Cruelty to Animals (KSPCA) pulled him from the river. He was a true

Heinze 57-variety handsome bush dog with, despite his confused ancestry, a raised line of hair along his back to do any pedigreed Rhodesian ridgeback proud.

Grotty, well he was grotty when rescued by the KSPCA, was a great watchdog and a loyal friend. But when Peter, the shamba man's adult daughter, made an unannounced visit, Grotty bit her. Peter was seriously upset.

"Grotty bit my daughter. He bit my daughter," he kept saying.

"Is she badly hurt?" I asked.

"No sir."

"Well I am sorry she was bitten Peter, but Grotty didn't know her and he would not have attacked her if you had met her at the top gate." That seemed to placate him and under my breath I muttered: "Thank God Grotty has had his rabies shots!"

Grotty loved the two little sausage dogs who would take it in turns to sit between his paws while he rid them of their fleas. If he paused to take a rest they would give him a little nip which was dog-speak for: get on with it Grotty, you haven't finished the job yet.

We acquired Zoe and Cleo when a friend, returning home, left us with them on permanent loan. They were eight months old at the time. Zoe was a traditional smooth-haired black and tan and Cleo a sandy coloured wire-haired. Unkindly, they call the wirehaireds dunny brushes in the doggy world.

Cleo was an absolute character. She would chase squirrels up trees and even climb after them if they the tree had a leaning trunk. And she would bark at chameleons and bumble bees. Once we heard her barking furiously at a small snake. Smart dog, she never tried to bite it. That was a job for mongooses. She was smart too in other ways and her party trick was when we doled out bones to all four dogs. Barking excitedly, she would race down to the back fence with the other dogs in hot pursuit. Then she would quickly double back and collect all the bones and bury them.

Zoe had a different temperament. Brave at times, but a real sook when the vet came on his annual visits to give the anti-rabies jabs. The vet would be barely at the top of the long driveway when Zoe sensed he was coming. Before you could say hot doggety do, she would give a series of piercing yelps and screams and hide in whatever sanctuary she could find: under beds, under couches and, if you hadn't shut the doors, in the garden. The following anonymous verse, sent to me by John Coldrey, a former justice of the Victorian Supreme Court, captures the essence of the sausage dog:

There was a dachshund oh so long,
he hadn't any notion
How long it took to notify
his tail of his emotion
And so it was that whilst his eyes
were filled with woe and sadness
His little tail went wagging
because of previous gladness

Brin, like Grotty, came from the KSPCA. We called him Brin because, well, he was a brindle dog. When we set eyes on him in the society's compound we couldn't resist the hopeful twinkle in his soft brown eyes.

But Brin was snappy at times, making us think that he had been ill-treated by a previous owner. If I had to guess I would say he was a Labrador cross and like a Lab, he was prone to growing fat. We fed him a normal diet but, unknown to us, he was sneaking off to the nearby police lines where the constables' wives and children would give him treats.

So Brin got fatter and fatter and his eyes began to fade. In the end he was totally blind but still managed to find his way to the police lines. Then one day, a friend dropped in to ask: "Have you seen your Brin today, because I think that's him lying dead on the road." Dark dog. Dark wet night. The driver would not have seen the dog — and blind Brin would not have seen the car that hit him. Peter got out the wheelbarrow and brought him back for a home burial.

When Diana and Imogen packed up for the flight back to Australia, they took the three remaining dogs to the KSPCA to await a new owner and home. It wasn't long before a well groomed Danish woman came, saw the two dachshunds, plus Grotty, in an enclosure and said, pointing to Zoe and Cleo:

"I'll take those two."

"Sorry," said Jean Gilchrist, the senior KSPCA officer, "it's a job lot. They all go or all stay."

"Okay," said the woman without hesitation," I will take all three."

So off they all went off to their new home.

Chapter 18

A BIRD'S LIFE

The bird life in Nairobi and indeed throughout Kenya is amazing. More than one 1000 species have been identified and recorded, making the country the eleventh top bird country in the world and the second in Africa behind The Congo. A twitcher's paradise.

In our backyard, the visitors included tiny, brilliant coloured sunbirds, dainty namaqua doves, malachite kingfishers, mannekin finches, odd-looking hamekopfs (so named because of the way their long bill and crest gave them a hammerhead look) and brownish-grey mousebirds with punk hairdos. Rather than stand upright on a branch, the mousebirds would often hang by their claws, with the rest of their bodies hanging down. Cute as they were, gardeners regarded them as pests because of the damage they wreaked on vegetable plots and fruit trees.

Then there were the large hadada ibis, so named after the way they would fly over crying a distinctive haa-haa-haa-de-dah. Their call had a spontaneous effect on our dogs. First Grotty would open up with long dingo-like howls, and then Brin and the two dachshunds would chime in with a sustained noisy chorus. Which was the signal for all the dogs in the neighbourhood to add voice to the din. Sometimes in the early morning you would find one or two Ibis in the garden probing for insects. They were attractive birds with a fluorescent greenish-purple sheen on their wings.

Barbecue time was the signal for black kites to put in an appearance. The kites had an uncanny ability to spot prey from a great height — and, I suspect an uncanny smell once the barbie had been lit and the sausages were sizzling away. In the beginning you would see a few specs idly circling in the sky. Then their numbers would increase once the cooking got under way.

A favourite party trick was to throw a sausage or piece of chicken into the air. The kites would quickly get the message and swoop down to grab the tasty morsels before they hit the ground. In quick time the sky would be thick with swooping kites. It became a dicey game, as the kites would sometimes take food clean off the plates that guests were holding. It was a dangerous practice and we soon put a stop to it.

Kenya is blessed with wildlife and like all newcomers to the country we set out to see — and saw — the so-called Big Five: lion, elephant, Cape buffalo, leopard and rhinoceros. But, contrary to public imagination, the most dangerous of these is not the lion, which kills fewer than 100 people a year, but the harmless looking hippopotamus. This almost comical, roly-poly killer, according to the *Mother Nature Network,* is responsible for about 2,900 deaths a year.[2]

This figure seems extraordinarily high, but reliable sources are hard to find. Tourists in Africa are warned not to get close to hippos on land, particularly if they find themselves between the hippos and their calves that wait in the water while their parents graze. Despite his lumbering appearance, a 1,500 kilogram male hippo (the name means *river horse*) can turn on a speed burst of nearly 32 kilometres an hour. And what a bite it has. A hippo has a cavernous mouth that may stretch from two feet wide at the lip up to a fearsome four or five feet when fully extended.

We had our own close encounter with a hippo at Lake Naivasha, a large fresh water lake in the Great Rift Valley, about 100 kilometres north-west of Nairobi. At the time, Diana's parents, John and Lorna Roberts, were visiting us and we packed them into the car and drove to the lake. The best way to see the lake is to hire a flat-bottomed boat and guide. Five of us — Diana, John, Lorna, daughter Imogen and myself — took our places in the boat and the skipper steered it out into deep water. The lake, and its surrounds, teems with bird life. Pelicans grace the water. Fish eagles soar above and pied kingfishers make sudden dives for small prey from trees lining the banks.

We rounded a bend and there, close to the shoreline, we saw our first group of hippos. There were a dozen or more, little ears wiggling away as they played hippo games of hide-and-seek. There were a number of youngsters in the group. We were delighted and asked the boatman if we could get a closer look. He cut the engine and glided in.

Bad move.

A big bull hippo, which had been watching us for some time with a malevolent eye, suddenly made a dash for the boat, creating a huge chest bow-wave as he accelerated.

No real need to worry. All the boatman had to do was pull the outboard rip cord and speed away.

He tugged at the cord.

No response.

He tugged again.

Nothing.

I remembered that John, my father-in-law, could not swim. Even in shallow and buoyant beach water, when he tried to float, he would sink. Like a stone.

The hippo was getting closer. If he reached us, he would shatter the boat or upturn it. We would all be drowned or chopped up by his huge jaws. We were on the edge of panic when the skipper, cool as a cucumber, pulled the cord for the third or fourth time. The motor burst into life and we sped away. The skipper had no doubts. He had gone through this routine hundreds of times.

After the hippopotamus, the Cape buffalo is one of the most dangerous of animals. People are inclined to regard it as some sort of exotic cow but, like the hippo, its moods are uncertain, and it kills about 200 people a year. In Africa, crocodiles also kill many people, as well as animals making their annual migration across the Serengeti and the Maasai Mara plains. The *National Geographic* magazine in 2005 put the human death toll at about 500 a year.[3]

Elephants sometimes kill people. In Kenya, the victims are usually farmers trying to protect their *shambas* from hungry tuskers that invade and destroy their crops. In a seven-year span 200 people died this way. But the tragic truth is that humans, profiting from the illegal ivory trade, are the real killers. Britain's

The Guardian newspaper in 2016 reported that elephants were being killed faster than they could breed.[4]

About 40,000 elephants are killed by poachers in Africa each year. That is, about one every 15 minutes. Thirty thousand of these killings take place in Kenya. It doesn't take rocket science to predict that, if the trend continues, this magnificent animal will soon be extinct. The only elephants you will see then will those in a zoo.

Kenya valiantly tries to get on top in the constant battle with poachers. During our stay, President Daniel Moi earned the plaudits of the world when in July, 1989, he put the torch to a 12,000-tonne stockpile of elephant tusks.

It was a dramatic, but futile gesture to halt or diminish the illegal ivory trade. In more recent times, Kenyan rangers have been shot and shot at many times. Between 2014 and 2017, thirteen have died in gun battles with poachers.

It is an uneven war. Countries such as China continue to buy the ivory and the rangers are out-gunned by an enemy with more powerful weapons. In addition, the poachers have GPS tracking and sophisticated mobile phone networks. They also have the odd helicopter according to one report.

However, in the animal kingdom, there is one killer that outstrips all others.

It weighs only 2.5 milligrams with a super-sized variety making 10 milligrams. And yet it is more powerful than a 7000 kilogram bull elephant.

It is the malarial mosquito.

In 2015, the World Health Organisation reported an estimated 214 million new cases of malaria and 438,000 deaths.

Ninety per cent of these deaths were in Africa, 292,000 of them children under the age of five. However there is cause for optimism: the WHO estimates that the death toll has dropped from about 800,000 in the year 2000 — a fall of about 70 per cent. This fall is attributed to better treatment, awareness and management.

During my time at the Nigerian Institute of Journalism, staff were often reporting sick with "the fever". Many of them did not take anti-malaria drugs, but opted for an injection after an attack. Many Kenyans also take the same approach.

Chapter 19

SAMMY SOUNDALIKE

My role at Nation Newspapers took a different direction to the one I had fulfilled in Nigeria. From teaching students, I was now training practising journalists at all levels. There were other differences too: The Press in Kenya was arguably more sophisticated than the Nigerian one and I had inherited an existing training system from my highly regarded predecessor, the Briton Bob Hitchcock.

I was told that Hitchcock's arrival at Nation House had been anything but welcoming among the editorial staff. Far from the grand entrance, he found himself unceremoniously dumped in the middle of the newsroom without an office and had to fend largely for himself. Which he did with aplomb, winning friends and influencing people in the best Dale Carnegie tradition.

One of the initial road blocks was the suspicion and animosity of the sensitive union representative, impatient for the complete Kenyanisation of the journalistic staff. Finally though, through dedicated hard work, Hitchcock won the respect of both the union and the newsroom.

Some of this mistrust of foreigners had lingered, however, when I joined the staff, despite being introduced in glowing terms by the Group Managing editor, George Mbuguss. At least I had an office, even sharing the services of a secretary with the Managing Editors of *The Daily Nation* and *Taifa Leo,* the Kiswahili newspaper.

I soon understood why talk of complete Kenyanisation, despite the company's clear policy to achieve this, was premature. The main obstacle was the poor grasp of English, partly due to how the African ear perceives the pronunciation of certain English words.

For instance, sometimes we would read *snickers* for *sneakers, buffled* for *baffled, buglary* and sometimes even *buggery* for *burglary, fanfare* for *funfair, rapture* for *rupture, breeding* for *bleeding* and many more. I called this syndrome "Sammy Soundalike". The examples above are reproduced in Gerard Loughran's splendid book *Birth of a Nation, the story of a newspaper in Kenya.*

Sammy Soundalike made many appearances and became quite a star in a weekly bulletin called *Let's Get it Right.* Started by Bob Hitchcock, it was an excellent guide to the sins of commission and omission that appeared regularly in the pages of *The Daily Nation* and *Sunday Nation.*

To supplement this I ordered an oversized scrapbook into which I pasted, and critiqued, examples of good and bad journalism — prose, introductions, headlines, design and lapses in grammar and syntax. I recall that on one occasion a sports feature contained about 70 mistakes. It amazed me how such a shoddy piece of work could get by the sports sub-editors and the proof readers. A senior editorial executive, on viewing my comments about the perpetrator, remarked: "But he's a university man!"

"Maybe," I replied, "but you wouldn't know it from this effort."

Most of the schoolboy howlers I had gleaned over nearly nine years were lost when I was forced to leave Kenya in mid-1994. But the following examples were fortunately resurrected and, recorded by Gerry Loughran in his book, give an accurate picture of the language difficulties I encountered. Such as the clichés "from which no self-respecting Kenyan journalist would ever be separated"; "sweet sweet-talking conmen"; "gun-totting (sic) police who swing into action"; and "leave no stone unturned". (Mind you, some of these clichés are not exactly unsighted in the Western Press.)

Loughran continues: "Tortured grammar, dodgy spelling, and mistaken idioms produce *rendering* for *rending, whooping* for *whopping, over-speeding, over-bleeding* for *over-breeding, in hot soup,* a *thorn in the neck, avail* for *made available, fled for his dear life, shed off* for *shed, a bush* for *the bush, pick* for *pick-up, flock the church, swarm the building, far more better* and trouble with compound nouns: *deadwoods, machineries, underwears.*" And so on and so on.

Life was tough for a training editor and even tougher for the sub-editors who had to make sense of it all. Frustrated, I took up the issue with George Mbuguss. His response: "How long has Australia been a nation?"

"About 200 years"

"Well, Kenya has been a nation for only 29 years," he replied.

Fair enough I suppose. He was saying that Kenya, like Rome, was not built in a day. But I felt it was a bit of a cop-out. As

Loughran points out, training was always a serious commitment of the *Nation* white hierarchy who had always had the goal of writing themselves out of a job.

Indeed, many *Nation* journalists — and there were some highly talented ones at the top — had benefited from early training schemes under the auspices of the International Press Institute (IPI) and other programs. Somewhere along the way, however, others had fallen by the wayside.

Apart from using such tools as *Let's Get it Right,* the *Plus and Minus Book* and the *Nation Style Book,* I ran regular training seminars in such places as Mombasa and Lake Naivasha. These were always popular, as much for the after-hours socialising as the instruction.

The road trips from Nairobi to Mombasa were hairy, dangerous and uncertain as to what to expect next — like the awesome and terrifying sight of two semi-trailers or two buses suddenly appearing on the crest of a hill. Abreast and on the wrong side of the road. The road was narrowed by sharp, broken edges. Ripped tyres and wrecked vehicles strewn by the roadside illustrated the carnage.

Kenya's road toll is one of the worst in the world. According to a new global survey by the World Health Organisation, 13,463 Kenyans died on the roads in 2017. This toll is four times higher than the government figure of 2,965 deaths. The WHO adds that deaths on the roads far exceed the global rate and is somewhat higher than the average for Africa. This huge discrepancy is blamed on a weak data base, rather than deliberate government under-reporting. Fortunately, I didn't drive my own car on these trips and my safety was in the hands of very capable drivers, either photographers or other staffers. The drive down was always packed full of interest. I remember a photographer pointing out the highlights:

"See that big house over there?"

"Yes."

"That belongs to a politician."

And a little further on:

"That mansion over there. That one's owned by a high-ranking minister in the government."

In Kenya, as in other parts of Africa, men (and they are mostly men) seldom enter politics for altruistic reasons, often using positions in business or sport to leverage their ambitions.

Family day out: Diana snapped this pride of lions on an earlier trip to the Mara.

Bevy of beauty. Imogen Lawrence with final-year colleagues from Hillcrest Prep.

Bill Young with the cheetah Duma.

Bush Baby Galago liked to nest in Bill Young's riding hat.

A real cuddle toy. Cheetah Siri shares a bed with Steve Meacher.

Robert Foster in the Main House at Sand Island Beach.
Note the trophy heads.

Francis (Fuzz) Foster in everyday garb takes it easy at home on Sand Island Beach.

The ebbing tide begins to reveal Sand Island south of Mombasa.

Sand Island homestead. The structure on top was salvaged from a shipwreck.

Partly hidden by tropical growth, this is believed to be a pen to hold slaves.

Friends of fur and feather. Chester the dog chums up with cat and eagle.

Three muskateers: Barry Henricksen, John Lawrence and Kern Roberts on the author's 60th birthday.

Diana's parents, Lorna and John Roberts, get to know Phil and Tim Tilley at the ranch.

Chapter 20

COAST CULTURE

Family trips to Mombasa and beyond were also full of interest. We would set the alarm for sparrow fart, pack up the car and set off early before the heat and traffic built up. We were always on the lookout for wildlife on the road to the coast. Poaching had not reached the species-threatening proportions of more recent times and we were delighted when, on one trip, we found the road blocked by a herd of seven elephants. We watched spellbound as the herd, unconcerned by our presence, took its time to disperse.

Nearer to Mombasa at Voi we ran the usual gauntlet of baboons that sat on top of the high granite outcrops and sometimes came down to pester tourists, clambering over cars, looking for food scraps and admiring themselves in the wing mirrors. You only have to look at the canine teeth of baboons to realise they would be nasty customers to tangle with. Leopards, it is said, rate them high on their culinary wish list, but I reckon a baboon would put up one hell of a fight.

Of real concern to us on the way down was the number of

women and men selling bags of charcoal — each bag representing the loss of a tree and a further blow to conservationists in their fight to save Kenya's dwindling forests.

According to a 2015 study by the non-government agency Green Africa Foundation, Kenya loses 5.6 million trees every day, "despite relentless campaigns on environmental conservation".[1]

The foundation says that, based on the 2009 national population census, there are 8.7 million households in Kenya. About 64.6 per cent of these depend entirely on firewood for cooking. Other causes of deforestation include commercial logging, cattle ranching, cash crop plantations and construction of dams, roads and mines.

Reaching Mombasa, a noisy, dirty city of about 1.2 million people, was always a relief, signalling that our hot, sweaty journey would soon be over.

Mombasa plays a key role in Kenyan culture, politics and history. Its roots go back nearly one thousand years, being variously ruled by the Omanis, the Portuguese and the British. It is the main port not only for Kenya, but also for the rest of the East Africa coast.

This region is the birthplace of the Swahili or Kiswahili language, which translates as "The language of the coast". Kiswahili is a properly constructed language and, with English, is the official language of the nation. There are both Swahili and English-language newspapers and magazines. Both languages are spoken in the National Parliament.

Most people who come to Kenya on short or long-term contracts pick up at least some Kiswahili, rejoicing in the use of such words as *kali* (meaning fierce as in a fierce man or woman or a fierce fire), *shenzi* (meaning uncouth or not quite proper; people refer to a shenzi dog — a mongrel) and *shamba* (meaning garden or small farm). Kiswahili has nothing in common with the pidgin of the West Coast except both — the structured and the ad hoc — were lines of communication between foreign travellers and traders.

Another language, *Sheng,* is stamping its authority among Kenya's urban youth, particularly among slum dwellers in Nairobi's Kibera and similar locations. It is a blend of Kiswahili and English, with creole and local languages thrown in for good measure. Very hip among the young, it is now moving into mainstream society.

According to an online article — *History and origin of Swahili* — published in 2012, Swahili existed as a genuine Bantu language even before the arrival of the Arabs. Many new words were added over the centuries, thanks to interaction between the inhabitants of the East African coast and Arabic, Indian and Persian traders, and the Portuguese invaders.

Chapter 21

ISLAND PARADISE

From Mombasa we would take the ferry for a 500 metres trip across Kilindini Harbour to Likoni, and then drive south to the beautiful beaches of Shelly, Tiwi and Diani. The ferry trip was an event in itself: An amazing assortment of ethnicities and merchandise, live and insensate.

And there were the irreverently named *buibui* or spider women. The word actually refers to the black cloth, worn as a shawl by Muslim women, and sometimes discreetly drawn across the eyes. From mainland Likoni it took about 35 minutes to drive the 22 kilometres to Sand Island on Tiwi Beach.

It was a first-you-see it and now-you-don't small island which came and went according to the tide. It was a great safe, shallow swimming spot for families thanks to a long reef that prevented sea surges. If you were more adventurous you could slip over the reef to snorkel or scuba-dive. From our rustic thatched roof cottage we would saunter down for an early morning swim or bargain for the fresh fish or octopus still wriggling on the spears of the local fishermen.

Meanwhile, back at the cottage, our assigned cook, Juma, would be preparing a breakfast of locally-grown tropical paw paw and mango, delicious with a squeeze of lime juice, followed by a full English breakfast of eggs, grilled tomato and sausage.

Sand Island Cottages were run by two white Kenyan brothers, Robert Foster, and his younger brother, John Francis (Fuzz) Foster. The Foster brothers'standard dress was shorts, sometimes a shirt, and no underpants, which could be eye-averting stuff when Robert sat down on our front porch wall for one of his regular chats. And they shaved under their arms.

Robert was a great hit with kids, showing them and explaining the history of the game-trophy heads hanging on the walls of the main house, picking small mangos for them which they ate by piercing the skin and sucking out the juice, and taking them on car trips to see wild animals.

Fuzz was more taciturn. He seldom spoke much, but hoped to make his fortune by growing aloe vera. He also developed a fine tropical orchard of citrus fruits, mangoes, pineapple, guavas, custard apples, sour sops and bananas.

This Sand Island Shangri-la was discovered by the Fosters' amazing mother, Zoe. Zoe was looking for a seaside family retreat, only to be told that just about all beachfronts had been snapped up. Undaunted she continued her search until she was tipped off that a vacant site was available at Tiwi beach.

But there was a problem: impenetrable scrub for about five kilometres barred access from the road. So Zoe set out to reach the site by walking and swimming along the coast. She swam most of the six and a half kilometres to avoid putting her feet down on the shallow sea bed where masses of prickly sea urchins lay in wait for the unwary. The swim paved the way for a successful claim on 122 acres which became the site for the cottages. Nearly 400 metres of this was pristine beachfront.

There were other pluses too as the site had sweet underground drinkable water and a rich earlier history as evidenced by a old slave pen and other artefacts from bygone times. Zoe was also a legend with her cooking skills, training up the small boys known as kitchen *totos*. Juma, our middle-aged cook, was one of her protégés.

Zoe was also an accomplished shooter, a dab hand with a speargun, a polo-playing horsewoman and a skilled self-taught artist. The main house at Sand Island had a feature wall displaying the 360 species of fish from the area, caught, identified and painted by Zoe and others.

After that swim, the Fosters set to clearing the scrub and creating a dirt road down to the beachfront. Hugh and his brother Fronny, Robert and Fuzz's father and uncle respectively, enlisted Teso tribesmen from Uganda to help them. The Teso were chosen because of the historic Foster connection with Uganda where they farmed and hunted for many years. And they also spoke the Teso dialect which was a huge help when it come to giving orders.

Perhaps it was a reflection of the times that Hugh Foster was the only one of 10 siblings who had children. Hugh died, aged 61, from cancer in 1956. Zoe also died from cancer, in 1961. She was only 57. Son Robert died, aged 75, in 2006. Fuzz, who wrote part of a book about the Foster family fortunes in Kenya, lived on until he was 83. He died in 2015. Their half sister, Neville, died in 2005.

It wasn't until early December 2018, that I finally caught up with Mary, the youngest and only surviving member of the Foster quartet. She now lives in Florida, USA, with Don Rooken-Smith, her husband of nearly 60 years.

Mary says she was never really interested, like others of the family, in shooting and fishing, but was a member of the famous mixed gender polo team. The team was all Foster — Robert, Fuzz, Neville and Mary. It seldom lost a match. Fuzz was a crack horseman and represented Kenya internationally in polo.

Mary, says husband Don, was brought up among "a bunch of apes". "Ever since she can recall, right up to her early teens, the Fosters of Kaptagat, had chimps around the house. The first chimp was Big Andy, who was not all that tame, followed by Little Andy, Stephen, and Sarah."

Stephen was a class act. Mary's mother, Zoe Foster, taught him to wear clothes, ride a tricycle, sweep the floor, get in and of bed and unlock a brass container to get his daily glass of milk. He could also, says Don, drawing on what Mary had told him countless times, "blow the most enormous and long-lasting cigarette smoke rings" and to light and blow out a candle. Stephen regularly sat down at the table and ate the same food as everyone else. See the appendix for the rest of the amazing Stephen the chimp story.

Day-by-day management of Sand Island during our time in Kenya, was in the hands of Samira Carey, a small, vivacious and attractive woman from the Island of Lamu. Samira had the energy of two men. She and husband, Pat, became our good friends. They now live in Sioux Falls, South Dakota, where Samira interprets for refugees.

Samira fondly recalls her time at Sand Island. In a recent email to me, she said: "I was manager in charge of the workers, the guests, the paperwork, the finances, the shopping, the selling of fruit from the orchard to hotels and Sand Island Beach guests.

"I enjoyed my 10 years working at Sand Island, like going to the office in my bikini, having fruit trees a few yards from my front door and the beach a few yards from my back door."

A great side trip from Sand Island was a foray into the Shimba Hills National Reserve. In less than two hours we found ourselves in a totally different environment and eco system. The original rainforests in much of Kenya are fast disappearing, but the reserve encompasses one of the largest coastal forests in East Africa.[1]

Kenya Wildlife Service audits list the following animals in the reserve: sable antelope (rare and endangered), elephant, giraffe, leopard, genet, civet cat, hyena, waterbuck, bush pig, African bush baby, bushbuck, the beautiful coastal black and white colobus monkey, blue duiker, bush duiker, red duiker, greater galago, black-faced vervet monkey, Sykes monkey, serval cat, black and red shrew and knob-bristled suni shrew. One hundred and eleven bird species have also been recorded.

Our journey into the hills had a touch of drama. Fiona, one of my daughters, was with us, along with Diana and Imogen.

We were driving along a narrow one-way dirt road when we came across a family of elephants. They were just off the road in the bush. There was the usual matriarch and her brood. A young bull elephant was looking directly at us and flapping his ears.

I stopped for a closer look. He started throwing up clouds of dust with his trunk. Diana was becoming a trifle nervous. Fiona recalls what happened next as the young bull looked like he was about to cross our path:

"Shit John, quick," shouted Diana. "He's coming our way."

"No rush," I said coolly.

"He's about to charge," said Diana. And he did!

"Right," I said, putting the gear into first and driving off at speed.

I glanced at the young bull in the rear vision mirror.

He looked disappointed.

Chapter 22

WARTHOGS GALORE

You never know with elephants. Another time we were staying overnight on safari in a Maasai Mara game park. The following morning, escorted by an armed ranger, we went on a bush walk. About 200 metres away we sighted a group of three large elephants on an almost treeless plain. One of the elephants seemed to resent our presence and made a few preliminary steps towards us. Diana was getting edgy.

"My little heart went pitter patter," she said afterwards. The warden sensed her anxiety.

"It's all right," he said calmly. You just clap three times and they will go away."

It sounded like African juju to me, particularly as the aggressive one edged a little closer and the others made moves to follow. Ears were flapping and the lead animal was throwing up dust. Not comforting signs.

Nowhere to run to. Nowhere to hide. Only a few hundred metres between us and the elephants. Good to his word, the warden clapped loudly three times and, amazingly, the aggressive elephant turned away and rejoined her mates. Nice trick, but I would not recommend it next time you go on safari.

The Mara is a treasure and can come up with all sorts of surprises. Such as the time we were on a conducted tour in one of those open top mini-buses that are such a feature — some would say unwanted feature — that crowd the Maasai Mara landscape at times. Others in the mini-bus with us were a new friend, Gail Gillespie from Brisbane, and Frank, a future novelist and would-be tennis player. We were looking for lions and soon found them in a most dramatic way.

Without warning the rear left wheel of the bus dropped suddenly into a warthog hole and in the next instant warthogs sprang out and sprinted in all directions.

Most made their escape, but a lioness and her half-grown cubs had been watching the incident with interest. One of the cubs tackled the hapless warthog and the other five piled on top like a rugby scrum.

We watched fascinated, not without sympathy for the warthog which was facing death by a thousand bites. However, just when all seemed lost, the warthog miraculously emerged from the mauling pack and staggered away. But the bid for freedom was shortlived. Mother lion took charge and with one swipe administered the *coup de grace*.

Chapter 23

MONGOOSE MAYHEM

Wild animals kept as pets were always popular with white settlers in East Africa. Mostly they were kept unchained and allowed to come and go as they pleased. The Fosters, in the pioneering days in Uganda before migrating to Kenya, were a good example. These were the parents, grandparents and other close relatives of Robert, Fuzz, Neville and Mary.

It was like an open air menagerie that included a gorilla, a leopard, ground hornbills, storks, a hyena and many mongooses, the latter of which were often taken on holidays. They made great pets and were a protection against snakes, as anyone who has read Rudyard Kipling's story about Riki Tiki Tavi, will attest.

The mongoose's sheer agility and speed means it can easily dodge as the snake strikes and wears itself out. It is are also unaffected by the snake's venom. As pets, they have a mischievous and sometimes temperamental streak. The Foster family's book, *Uganda Adventures,* recounts the habit of one pet mongoose whose party trick was to dash out of cover and nip visitors on the heel.

Then, before you could say Jack Robinson, it would dash back to its hiding place. It also took great delight in ambushing and tormenting the family cat by giving it a quick nip as it lazed, unsuspecting, in the sun. It was a wonderful game. If you were a mongoose.

Years later, while on holiday at Sand Island, Robert Foster introduced us to a pet mongoose that they housed in an enclosed run. When Imogen tried to give it a pat the mongoose bit her finger. It was not a friendly nip and despite being reassured by Robert that Imogen would be okay, we lived in fear of the dreaded rabies virus for some time. The World Health Organisation says the incubation period for rabies is typically one to three months but can vary from one week to a year.

Wild mongooses wreaked havoc back at our home in Nairobi, breaking into the *kuku kidogo* (bantam chooks) pen to create mayhem and murder. It happened in the middle of the night when we were awakened by an unholy din. A battle-scarred and bloodied rooster, which had tried valiantly to protect the little hens, was strutting around the lawn in a defiant punch-drunk manner. Grotty, the dog, was also awakened by the din, and was stalking the rooster.

And as Peter the shamba man tried to rein in Grotty, the rain poured down. Imogen, who also been awakened by the din, was yelling: "Can't anyone get any bloody sleep around here." *Kuku kidogo* are cute little fowl and good egg-layers, but enough was enough. The surviving hens had to go. We donated them to Florence the housekeeper, who gratefully received them. A few months later she told us that, looked after by her mother, they were not only laying, but hatching many chickens as well.

Chapter 24

DOWN ON THE RANCH

One of the great events on our social calendar was the annual cricket match at the Athi River Game Ranch, some 35 kilometres south-east of Nairobi. It was a challenge between a rag-tag Nairobi team, which I captained, and the Athi River side, skippered by either ranch manager Phil Tilley, an Australian, or Dr David Hopcraft, the owner of the property.

There was no oval as such. For that matter, there was no cricket pitch. But, necessity being the mother of invention, Phil quickly overcame such trifling details. To make an oval was surprisingly simple: Phil roughed out the dimensions of an oval and then hopped on a mower to delineate the playing area.

There were no boundary lines; the boundary began where the short grass ended. Next, the pitch: Phil co-opted a small army of African staff who mattocked, hammered and rolled out a respectable wicket that stood the test of time. However, there was a complication. The oval was also the ranch's air strip. Which added a degree of uncertainty and excitement at critical times in a match.

It was limited over cricket. Everyone had to bat and everyone had to bowl. Except the wicket-keeper. There were frequent pauses for drinks in the outfield where players sometimes brought cans of beer on to the ground. A sumptuous lunch, rustled up by some of our Indian friends, was the highlight between innings. They were some of the best curries Diana and I had ever had. Being the captain I opted to open our side's batting — not because I was any great shakes as a cricketer, but because I could soon get back to the marquees and partake of a civilised drink or two. Meanwhile the air sock on the airstrip/cricket ground fluttered proudly in the breeze.

"What happens," I asked Phil, "if a pilot wants to land while a game is being played."

"Well," said Phil, "he lands, transacts his business and flies off again."

As if to read his mind, this came to pass all too suddenly at one of our matches. There was a cry of "plane coming in" and a light aircraft, escorted by a curious marabou stork, neatly skimmed over the stumps for a perfect landing.

Players smartly scurried from the field as the plane taxied to a halt. The pilot casually sauntered over to the marquees and addressed the intrigued cricket fans.

"I say, do the Trollopes live around here?"

"No," replied Phil pointing, "they live a couple of Ks down that away."

"Oh righto," said the pilot, spurning offers of a drink, "toodleoo then" and resumed his mission to find the Trollopes.

Shortly before our departure from Kenya, Diana had the bright idea to have a trophy made, for which the opposing teams would compete. A suitable small rock was found and a metal plate affixed to it. The inscription read something like "The Lawrence Memorial Trophy". Not be outdone, another character had a special T-shirt made for me. The front read AFRICA. And the back said REJECT. I keep it in a bedroom drawer and every now and then take it out and give it shake. It's a sentimental reminder of some very happy years.

The game ranch, an internationally renowned $80 million property owned by Dr David Hopcraft, owes much of its success to Phil Tilley, a South Australian engineer and self-styled "Mr Fixit" who has managed it for the past 40 years. The ranch is spread over 20,000 acres on the Athi Kapiti plain 1700 metres above sea level.

From 1980 to 2003 the ranch produced game meat for the Kenyan market. This included wildebeest, hartebeest, zebra, Thompson's gazelle, Grant's gazelle, impala, ostrich, eland (which makes a wonderful forequarter roast), oryx, waterbuck and giraffe. Phil, the perennial Mr Fixit, designed and built the slaughter house and cool room. Pressure from international animal rights groups saw the eventual banning of game meat.

Game meat aside, the ranch is a wonderful microcosm of the wildlife which once teemed on these plains. "We also host," said Phil, "cheetah, hyena, jackal, duiker, dik dik (a tiny antelope), aardvark, hyrax, zorilla, spring hare, serval cat, genet cat, leopard, striped hyena, bush babies, vervet monkeys, baboon and — at last count — 318 bird species."

Since the ban on game meat sales, the ranch has had to diversify. Today it concentrates on cattle-ranching, hay-making, eco-tourism, house rental and vehicle and farm equipment repair.

Scientists carry out research on the property and the ranch has been a popular locale for movie makers.

Another Aussie, Stuart Barden, a Nuffield scholar from Gilgandra in New South Wales, is causing great excitement in Athi River with experimental cropping on 3000 acres of unirrigated low rainfall soil. Phil says the entire Kenyan farming community is watching with interest. So far, he has successfully grown sorghum, barley, wheat, chic peas, green grams and maize on land which has just 500mm of annual rainfall.

How Phil Tilley landed the job on the ranch is a story in itself. In 1976 he and a friend bought a diesel Land Rover, equipped it with extra fuel tanks, and set off on a 21-month odyssey from London. They visited Morocco, Algeria, drove through Sahara desert to Niger and Nigeria and then on to Timbuktu, Mali, Upper Volta, Ghana, Liberia, Togo, Benin, Cameroon, Central African Republic, Zaire, Rwanda and Tanzania before resting up in Kenya for two months.

In early 1978 they headed south reaching Botswana and their destination of Cape Town, South Africa. "Neither of us felt comfortable in apartheid South Africa," Phil told me. "But we had really enjoyed Kenya, so we headed north again via Namibia, the Kalahari Desert, Okavango swamp and back to Mombasa."

They took a month to "tidy up the Land Rover "and finally reached Nairobi in July, 1978. They parked the Land Rover outside the main post office and attached a for sale sign. Two days later along came David Hopcraft who showed interest in the vehicle, invited the two adventurers to the farm and asked Phil to stay a while and help him out on the ranch. Forty years later Phil is still on the ranch, but thinking of retirement.

The ranch is part of a strip of land allocated to European settlers by the British in the 1920s. Its aim was to create business for the Mombasa to Nairobi railway, the so-called Lunatic Express which saw thousands of workers die during construction.[1] It was also meant to act as a buffer between the Wakamba and Maasai tribes.

Today storm clouds throw a shadow of uncertainty over the future of the ranch. Phil told me that 2017 was a terrible year for Kenya. He pointed to the invasion of many ranches in the north and the lack of decisive government action to deal with it. This, he said, had made a significant impact on many of the remaining ranchers and the political turmoil surrounding the 2017 elections had caused further nervousness. There is, of course, the fact that the ranch's close proximity to Nairobi and the seat of Government remains a tempting prospect for takeover and sub-division.

At the game ranch, a succession of cheetahs were the favourite pets. They became quite tame, but were essentially wild animals and allowed to roam the ranch at will and kill game for food. Our first close up and personal encounter with a cheetah was with Duma, a big male who got on well with both people and domestic pets. He was good pals with one of the Tilley dogs. But when it got too cheeky and invaded Duma's personal space, a friendly swipe of the big cat's paw made it clear who was boss.

You could pat and stroke Duma who would purr like a Formula One car engine and lick you with a tongue that felt more like a rasp. Duma was fitted with a sort of GPS collar that tracked his movements. There came a time when Duma failed to show up the ranch door and staff traced him to where the last call was heard. The splendid Duma had run his course. He was dead.

The next pet cheetah at the ranch was a feisty, frisky but friendly young female. We met her when we visited the ranch with our friends the Roberts family. Imogen and the Roberts' daughter, Bethan, approached the cheetah intending to give it a pat or a loving hug. Unfortunately for them the cheetah thought this was some sort of contact sport and jumped up playfully — the signal for two terrified girls to run screaming towards the house with the cheetah chasing. They clambered to safety by climbing up some outdoor sporting equipment and the cheetah, suddenly bored with the game, gave up the chase.

In retrospect it was really quite comical, a bit like an old-time slapstick movie. The sobbing girls, though, were anything but amused.

Steve Meacher, a teacher and conservationist who lived on the property, had a cheetah called Kiri, which he would take for regular strolls. In the picture pages you will even see Steve reading in bed, with Kiri snuggled up beside him. The way wild animals and domestic animals sometimes mix in harmony has always intrigued me. Also in the pictures section you will see the unusually grouping of a dog, a cat and a vulture.

Steve, an Englishman, and a Canadian, Bill Young, both now resident in Australia, lived on the ranch in Twiga (giraffe) House. Both were devoted conservationists who, like so many people before them, fell in love with the country's people and fauna.

"We'd both been mad about Africa in our childhoods, reading books, watching any TV doco we could," Bill, a hair consultant, told me in a recent email.

"The ranch was a great and interesting story by Hopcraft and Team. Its groundbreaking work in sustainable yield game meat proved that game are much more productive, and leave a smaller footprint, especially on marginal dry land like Athi, than cattle, sheep and goats.

"Twiga House, where we lived for seven or eight years, was originally built for a Swiss film maker planning to do a movie of the farm and its work. When the house became available we snapped it up. We faced Lukenya Hill to the north and to the south, on a very clear day, we could see the beautiful snow-capped Mount Kilimanjaro."

According to local legend, strange things can happen as one passes around the foot of Lukenya Hill along the Nairobi-Mombasa Road. Mystical forces play havoc with motorists, causing their cars to veer suddenly off course. Drivers, the myth says, lose all control and are helpless as they are pulled this way and that. But it remains just that. A myth. Diana and I have driven by the hill many times and nothing has happened. The mountain imps have smiled kindly. You will not find anything about the legend in the travel brochures and today the Lukenya Hills (to use the formal name) are a vibrant tourist getaway.

Bill and Steve became totally immersed in farm life and, when their day jobs in Nairobi allowed, nursed and adopted orphaned animals. There was Siri, the cheetah cub they cared for until she was placed with another ranch, Asali, a wildebeest calf, a duiker (small antelope) with a broken leg and many other animals and birds. And then there was Ziggy, the bushbaby "who used to sleep in our riding hats during the day and had to be gently ejected if we wanted to go riding".

Today, Bill and Steve live in Victoria, Australia. Bill, an expert in hair replacement techniques, and Steve, a long-time champion of animal welfare, is chairman of the Friends of Leadbeater Possum, a group fighting to save the tiny marsupial, Victoria's fauna emblem, from the destruction of its habitat by forest loggers.

*

Australians have long been involved in dryland research and experiment in sub-Sahara Africa. During our sojourn in Kenya, we got to know Dr Roger Jones, who was part of an expert team working at Machacos, 33 kilometres from Athi River. The team was assembling a wide selection of legume seeds and adapting them to varied farming systems in the Machakos and Kitui districts. It aimed to assist agronomists and animal production scientists in evaluating the seeds in on-farm experiments.

The work involved close collaboration between staff of the Kenya Government Ministry of Agriculture and staff of the Australian Dryland Farming Project. It was implemented by the CSIRO Division of Tropical Crops and Pastures. The experiments were carried out at four fenced sites in a range of climatic conditions with rainfall varying from 595 to 1179 mm.

Roger, and his wife, Anne, were active in church affairs in Nairobi. They were delightful dinner hosts, proving both fine food and wine and entertaining conversation. One of those dinner parties had unexpected consequences.

We were all nice and mellow when Anne got up and went to the bathroom. In the next instant, there was a scream. Roger and Diana rushed out to find that Anne had slipped and fallen awkwardly. Her ankle was fractured and bone was protruding through the skin.

Roger emerged from the bathroom to ring for a doctor and called out: “It’s now two down. You better see to your own wife.” Diana, shocked at the sight of the injured Anne, had fainted.

Chapter 25

THE WEZIES ATTACK

Fast forward to 1998 — four years after our departure — and Phil Tilley was celebrating his 50th birthday in style with, as one guest put it, Athi River royalty. It was the classic long lunch, extending well into the night.

One of those guests was Barry "Bazza" Henricksen, an Australian scientist working for the United Nations Environment Program. Phil and his wife, Tim, aware of the dangers of late night attacks by robbers, invited Barry and his wife, Robyn, to stay the night at the ranch. Barry, faced with the prospect of an early morning work start, declined.

It was a decision that nearly cost them their lives. Their drive home, via the Mombasa Road and the Kiambu Road, was uneventful until they reached their turnoff in Kiambu. Barry nosed the Land Rover onto the *murram* (dirt) road leading to their house. The location, about 13 kilometres from Nairobi, is relatively isolated. Several African and foreign neighbours had been attacked there in their cars over the years.

Barry gives a vivid description of what happened next.

"Unbeknown to us, a bunch of *wezies* (thugs or thieves) were hiding in the coffee plantation to our right. They had constructed an impressive bridge of large logs across the road and camouflaged it with vegetation, barring access 100 metres from our front gate. "We felt a sudden chill down the spine. Robyn was first to react and yelled 'Let's get out of here.' Barry threw the car into reverse and gunned it backwards in retreat.

"All hell broke loose," recalled Barry. "The driver's window shattered first, then the side window, both exploding into the car." Shadowy figures emerged from the plantation and, running to keep pace with the retreating car, began to hurl rocks. Just as Barry thought he had outpaced the first wave of attack, he felt a painful blow to his back and was temporarily winded. Then, increasing speed, and still in reverse, the Land Rover became unstable, left the track and landed in a muddy drain, facing at right angles to the road.

"As providence would have it," said Barry, "we had settled opposite the front gate of a neighbour's house. I slammed the accelerator down to clear the ditch."

Nothing happened.

"We could hear the Wezies shouting and running towards us again. I pumped the accelerator maybe 10 times. The Rangie let out a V8 bellow that would have awakened the dead. The engine coughed and spluttered."

And rolled back into the ditch.

"It was then that we became aware of a shadowy figure racing towards us. He was just 30 metres away. There he was, a fast-moving silhouette in the starlight. He was a bad guy with a very large rock and malicious intent and we were the object of his discontent."

Barry and Robyn had almost given up hope when the Range Rover suddenly fired up again and roared out of the ditch.

"We were now headed full steam ahead for the neighbour's gate, a substantial-looking structure with large rustic gate posts on either side of the entrance." The thug hurled his rock, which bounced harmlessly off the back of the car just as Barry drove straight at the gate. The fence posts snapped off, releasing the gate which sailed clean over the car. The assault on the gate scattered the watchdogs that had come out all fangs bared.

Barry sped the Land Rover across the lawn, all lights blazing and spun it around to so that it faced his attackers. But the bad guys had fled. "Then a flashlight flickered tentatively in our direction. It was one of the house staff coming out to see what the ruckus was all about." Someone hit the panic button and the security service people were on their way. Sometime later the *askari,* assigned by a security firm to guard the property, climbed down from the tree in which he was hiding.

"He had apparently been sleeping up there and had no wish to put himself in harm's way," said Barry. X-rays next day at the Aga Khan Hospital showed that Barry had escaped with a couple of broken ribs. Robyn, despite a case of the shakes, escaped uninjured.

Chapter 26

MAURITIUS

In 1988, with my first home leave looming, I was approached by the London-based Commonwealth Journalists Association to deliver the first formal journalism training in the Indian Ocean nation of Mauritius. Although some 2000 kilometres off the southeast African coast, the island is a member of the African Union.

The course was to last a month, which dovetailed nicely with my Kenya leave time. Diana and Imogen stayed the first week, then went on to Australia. I was greeted with great warmth by the Mauritians, but felt almost overwhelmed when I learned that I had 70 eager participants. I solved the problem by splitting the trainees into two equal groups — 35 beginners in the morning class and 35 practising journalists in the afternoon class.

It was an A to Z basics course, taking in everything from reporting, story construction and interviewing to newspaper layout and design. The course was strongly supported by the Government which sent along its information officers.

Mauritius in the 1980s was an absolute delight, an island of about a million people, the most densely populated country in Africa. You could play an absorbing game with yourself as you walked the quaint narrow streets, trying to guess and link faces to races. It's a cliché, but Mauritius is truly an ethnic melting pot, a throwback to the early sugar plantation years: African slaves, indentured Indian labourers, Chinese traders and the French and English who ruled them.

For a long time, the island was uninhabited. The Portuguese dropped in for an early 16th century visit, followed later by the Dutch who stayed around for about 70 years. But the two main players were the French, who ruled from 1715 until the British kicked them out in 1810 during the Napoleon wars. Although the British were the colonial masters until independence in 1968 — a period of 158 years — the French influence remains stronger.

I was told many Mauritians felt that in all those years Britain had done little for the development of the country. Although English is the official language, French is common and Creole is the patois that links the ethnic groups. During my stay in 1988, the main economic pursuits were sugar, woollen textiles and tourism. From the air you could see huge piles of volcanic rocks that had been cleared to make way for the sugar plantations. Today, thanks to migration, the biggest ethic group is Indian and predominantly Hindu.

My mentor and course co-ordinator was Beekrumsing Ramlallah, aided by his daughter, Sadhna. "Mr Ramlallah" — I don't think I ever called him by his first name of Beekrumsing, and certainly never Beek for short but, as I later learned, he was Beekrum to his friends.

He was one of the most charming, courteous and cultured

men I have met. One of our daily delights was during the lunch break when Mr Ramlallah would shout me to a bottle or two of cold Tiger beer as we discussed everything from the progress of the course itself to Mauritian politics and the social and cultural life of the island.

Beekrum was a famous figure in Mauritus: a teacher, a parliamentary secretary in the Health Ministry (and briefly a minister). He founded the Mauritius Union of Journalists and in 1954 set up the English language newspaper, the *Mauritius Times.*

A graduation ceremony followed the end of the one-month course. I felt humbled and overwhelmed when students and staff dug deep to shower me with gifts, including a solid brass Dodo and a fully rigged replica in miniature of a Dutch ship that once sailed Mauritius waters. Afterwards, Beekrumsing Ramlallah asked me if would like to set up and run a full-time journalism course. Sadly, because of the big difference in pay scales between Mauritius and Australia, I had to refuse.

It was the last time I saw Beekrum. He died, aged 85, on 12 September in the year 2000. Tributes paid to him on his death described him as a vigorous defender of free speech and a champion of the poorest and weakest segments of society.

Chapter 27

DINKY DI AUSSIE

Down Dingo. Down! The man with the distinctive Australian accent shouted as his blue heeler dog bounded up and licked us to death. We were in the tea district of Limuru, about 35 kilometres from Nairobi, and the man with the Aussie accent was Harold White, long-term Kenya resident and member of the famous White family.

White family roots in Kenya go back to 1919 when Major H.A.D. (Bert) White, DSO, settled in the Highlands. The major had brought a herd of Ayrshires with him, the first cattle to be brought from Australia, swimming them from boat to shore at Mombasa. Later he switched to beef cattle, becoming one of the country's leading Boran breeders.

Harold, one of his three sons, first visited Kenya with his father when he was just six. After an education in Australia, he returned 13 years later at the age of 19, working his passage from Sydney to Durban by looking after a flock of 86 merino sheep.

His nephew Geoffrey, Australia's High Commissioner when

we first arrived in the country, picks up the narrative in his biography *Harold Duckett White. An Australian Settler in Kenya:*

"After he delivered (the sheep) to their destination at Pietermaritzburg he went back to Durban and took a ship to Mombasa. He was met by his father on arrival on 8 September 1927 and, because there were no operational wharves, they were rowed ashore. Later they took the train to Nairobi and the start of Harold's long association with the Kenya Highlands."

Harold, like his father, became a pioneer. He was a director of the Kenya Co-operative Creameries and several other companies. In our time in the country, he lived at Limuru with his wife Daphne. A larger-than-life character, he was a frequent visitor to Australian High Commission events. He was a great talker and a great drinker.

Entertaining us at his home in Limuru, he would stand for an hour or two behind an occasional table, on which were placed a bottle of gin or vodka and a bottle of water. Both would progressively go down as he regaled us with stories past and present.

Harold was a fine figure of a man with a strong upright stance; even in his eighties, he would dive into a swimming pool, rather than dip a toe in first and gently wade in, as many men of his age would do. He was a keen follower of politics: Kenyan, international and Australian and for years he would religiously tune in to Alistair Cooke and his long-running weekly commentary *Letter from America.*

Australian politics fascinated him and he would often ask me: "How's the Goanna going, John?" This was a reference, of course, to the billionaire Kerry Packer who was code-named "The Goanna" by the *National Times* newspaper to protect his identity at the Costigan Royal Commission into the Australia's Painters and Dockers Union. Packer later admitted that he was indeed the Goanna.

Despite his many decades in Kenya, Harold never lost his Australian accent — and he never lost his identity as an Australian. He would go home eventually, he said. "When I am in my dotage."

But Harold never made it home. His son Peter, a Sydney solicitor, told me that a group of young thugs broke into his house and viciously assaulted Harold. All they got for their trouble was an old TV and an old radio. Harold spent time in hospital and, although making a limited recovery, died on 13 January 2002 from his injuries. He was 95. A good friend.

Harold wasn't the only White we met in Kenya. Geoffrey, his High Commissioner nephew, was the son of Geoff White Senior, another of the Major's offspring. The elder White arrived in Kenya for a holiday in 1946 when young Geoffrey was six — and stayed to practise law and farm.

As a diplomat, Geoffrey made a big hit when he presented his credentials to President Daniel arap Moi. Half-way through his speech, Geoffrey switched suddenly from English to fluent Swahili.

"President Moi got the shock of his life, but he was absolutely thrilled," Geoffrey told me when I interviewed him for the *Daily Nation* in March 1986. Later that year, Moi recalled that speech when he told a visiting Australian parliamentary delegation:

"I want to thank you for sending this man to this country. In some ways he knows more about it than we do. We are very pleased to have him." It was a home-coming for Geoffrey White after a 36-year absence. He was schooled in Kenya and did his obligatory army service there.

He remembers spending a night in the forests of the Aberdares, armed only with a .303 rifle. It was the early 1950s and the time of the bloody Mau Mau uprising. Geoffrey was just 18. Every sound, every call of animals, every snap of a twig and sigh of wind played on his nerves and imagination.

The Mau Mau revolt remains a sensitive issue. Thirty-two white settlers, 200 British police and soldiers, more than 1,800 African civilians and many thousands of rebels died.

Geoffrey White left Kenya in 1956 for Cambridge where in graduated in law. His subsequent diplomatic posts included Ottawa, Singapore and Saigon. But he still remembers his early school days and a visit to Nakuru in the Rift Valley when the colonial provincial commissioner (ostrich-plumed hat and all) would deal out a crate of apples to students.

"You look at the red part there," he would say, pointing to an apple. "That's symbolic of the British Empire."

In 1956, just short of his 18th birthday, the future High Commissioner found himself 11,000 feet up in the Aberdare Mountains with the Kenya Regiment in its fight against the Mau Mau, a bloody uprising which started in 1952 and ended in 1960.

He had been called up for National Service and his admission to Cambridge temporarily put on hold. In a family memoir, Geoffrey wrote:

"The worst years of the Mau Mau threat were over and only two of their military leaders were still out in the forests. One was the notorious Dedan Kimathi who was finally caught (and later hanged) after being wounded in late October 1956.

"We were essentially engaged in mopping up operational work. At the end of 1956, the Kenya Regiment was stood down and it reverted to being a territorial unit."

In those days, said White, the Mau Mau were called *terrorists* and *gangsters*. When he returned to Kenya in1982, the usual term was *freedom fighter*.

Geoffrey went on two operations in the Kinangop high country forests seeking out Mau Mau. In 1956, he reported in his memoir, there were an estimated 1500 Mau Mau guerrillas in the Aberdares and a similar number in the forests of Mount Kenya. This was well down from the more than 10,000 in the early phase of the Emergency.

In a letter to his parents in early May 1956, he gave this description of an operation near the Rift Valley escarpment:

"There are two fairly large gangs under hard core leaders who have been there since the beginning; one gang is seven and the other 13. In addition there are another 30 or 40 terrorists or sympathisers.

"Patrolling is tough. Up at 3am and back at 9 so our movements are mainly concealed by darkness. Other patrols go out at 10pm and return at 3am. We came back yesterday from Operation Royal Flush having spent two weeks in the Ndenya location near the escarpment. Eight terrorists were captured and five killed, including the big leader "General" Jimminji who was shot by *pseudos* (a gang) who did a marvellous job."

In another letter to his parents, Geoffrey White gives a good description of the mountainous terrain in which the Mau Mau battles were fought, as well as an idea of the plentiful wild life:

"I am now somewhere in the Aberdare forests just under Fay's peak. Patrolling is very hard as the altitude is quite high. On patrol you can go from 9,000 to nearly 10,000 feet. The highest point on the range is Satima at 13,210 feet. We are now close to the Talaga River where the riverbanks are steep.

"I have seen lots of Colobus monkeys and what beautiful animals they are. We have been on Kipipiri which has a height of 10,987 feet. We have been operating there between 10,000 and 11,000 feet looking for 40 terrorists. We have, however, found nothing as the Micks (the Mau Mau) are too clever these days and live most of the time closer to the towns.

"We met a lot of wild game including rhino, elephant, buffalo and bush buck. It was very wet and every night my sleeping bag was soaked right through and what with wet clothes you cannot feel warm, particularly at night."

The Mau Mau uprising, officially called The Emergency, was, and I guess still is, a sensitive topic during our tenure in Kenya. However, on 7 April 2011, the BBC reported that it was now regarded in Kenya "as one of the most significant steps towards a Kenya free from British rule. Most of the Mau Mau guerrillas came from the Kikuyu tribe with some support from the Embu and Meru.

The BBC's story (*Mau Mau uprising: Bloody history of Kenya conflict*) continued: "More than a million strong, by the start of the 1950s the Kikuyu had been increasingly economically marginalised as years of white settler expansion ate away at their land holdings. By 1952 Kikuyu fighters, along with some Embu and Meru recruits, were attacking political opponents and raiding white settler farm and destroying livestock. Mau Mau supporters took oaths, binding them to their cause."

Numbers killed in the conflict vary widely. Officially, says the BBC, 11,000 Mau Mau and other rebels were killed and 1,090 convicts hanged by the British administration. Only 32 white settlers were killed.

The Kenya Human Rights Commission tells another story: It alleges that "90,000 Kenyans were executed, tortured or maimed, and 160,000 detained in appalling conditions."

Chapter 28

THE PAPER WARS

The *Daily Nation* was launched on 20 March 1960, just three years after the declaration of independence. Its stable mates, *The Sunday nation* and the Kiswahili daily *Taifa Leo* were published earlier.

The story of the *Nation* is that of a newspaper that took on the establishment, particularly the white settler establishment, and won. And despite government attacks and opposition paper dirty tricks, survived and flourished. Furthermore, it had a powerful backer, founder and owner — the famous and flamboyant Aga Khan the Fourth, leader of the Ismaili Muslim sect and its 1.5 million adherents in 25 countries.

The elevation of the then Prince Karim as leader of the Ismailis was something of a shock, as his father, the notorious playboy Aly Khan, was the logical successor to the third Aga Khan. But the old Aga, unhappy with his son's excesses, skipped a generation and named Karim as his heir. The new Aga Khan's right-hand man and creative brain in the birth and development of the paper, was Michael Curtis, former Editor of Fleet Street's

News Chronicle. According to Mihir Bose, author of the meticulously researched *The Aga Khans,* Curtis over the years "was able to build up an efficient PR team, to shield the young Karim and promote his image".[1]

I met Michael Curtis on a couple of occasions when he came to Nairobi from the Aga Khan's headquarters in Aiglemont, France, on one of his inspection tours. He was tall, cultured and charming, but with the hard edge of the successful newspaper executive. He was also old-fashioned and courteous and always replied to letters in his own handwriting on personalised home address letterhead.

Cambridge University educated, Curtis was wounded in 1943 during the North Africa campaign. He died, aged 84, from cancer on 3 July, 2004.

Next to Curtis, the Aga Khan's most trusted lieutenant was the Irishman Gerry Wilkinson, who joined the group in 1971 as marketing manager before rising to general manager and a seat on the company's board. Despite harassment and personal attacks by politicians and the smugness of the white man's paper, *The East African Standard,* the Nation moved into profit in only eight years and overtook the *Standard* a year later.

It won the circulation war by driving to all corners of the nation, despite a vicious campaign of dirty tricks by the *Standard.* Or to use Curtis's words, it was "a good old-fashioned circulation war".

Gerry Loughran gives a blow-by-blow account of how the war was won in his book *Birth of a Nation.* He credits two men — Wilkinson and fellow Irishman Paddy Kearney — with spearheading the successful campaign.

Kearney supplied the local knowledge and Wilkinson drew on his experience as marketing manager with the *Irish Independent* in Dublin. Kearney was the Nation's circulation manager. Loughran says that Kearney, a former assistant police commissioner for Rift Valley Province, spoke fluent Kiswahili "and knew virtually every square inch of Kenya and many of its movers and shakers".

The *Standard* had a narrow strategy that concentrated on the cities, but Kearney outfoxed them by targeting the small towns and upcountry villages. When Diana and I arrived in Kenya in January, 1986, the story of how the war was won was still a topic of conversation in the newsroom. Kearney, as quoted in *Birth of a Nation,* tells how it was done:

"That was where we broke them, by opening up new rural areas and finding our own distributors. The local distributors were usually Africans and often we looked for disabled people. We took great chances on them but they were brilliant. They employed *totos* (children) wanting one cent or two cents a paper and those kids went to all the shopkeepers who were only too pleased to get the *Nation* on their doorstep. They took hundreds of papers to tiny villages and it cost us relatively little. There was one seller on Ngong Road, Kamau. We gave him, say, 600 papers and he had 10 or 12 *totos* delivering them to individual houses, about 400 of the 600. We went to places like Ravine, Molo, Embu, Nyeri, Karatina, Thika. We put vendors near bus stops. We were building a mass readership. The *Standard* never seemed to realise that Europeans were a declining readership.

In 1968, just a few years after its launch, the *Daily Nation* had overtaken the *Standards*' maximum sales mark of about 34,000.

And thanks to the drive, initiative and marketing skills of Gerry Wilkinson, it wasn't long before the *Nation* had overtaken the *Standard's* lead in classified advertising. By the time I arrived in January 1986 the daily circulation had soared past 150,000.

The *Daily Nation* was frequently attacked by the autocratic President Daniel arap Moi as a tool of the former colonial masters, pointing to the Aga Khan's outright ownership. It was both inaccurate and unfair considering the Ismaili leader's investment in the country. He had provided, among other things, both a leading school and a hospital, attending to the health and educational needs of thousands on Kenyans.

The Aga Khan neatly took the heat out of the issue by launching a public share float that reduced his holding to 44.7 per cent. Other large investors secured 13.6 per cent and the rest was taken up by the *wananchi* (the people).

Florence, our housekeeper, was delighted. "Sir," she said, barely containing her excitement, "I have just bought 2000 *Nation* shares." Technically, but utterly implausibly, the Aga Khan could be outvoted, but only if all the other shareholders ganged up on him. The spread of shares among the populace meant this would never happen. But it was a big statement as well as a clever manoeuvre by the Ismaili spiritual leader. Since our departure, the Nation group has become a multi-media conglomerate with a radio (music, news and talk-back), television and a string of magazines and newspapers. The group has more than 1,600 employees.[2]

Chapter 29

VALE DAME DAPHNE

I was putting the finishing touches to this book when I learned of the death of Daphne Sheldrick, of one of the most remarkable women of her time. Daphne, who died on 12 April 2018, was credited with saving 230 orphaned baby elephants in Kenya and paving the way for similar success in other parts of the world.

Daphne, or to give her full title, Dr Dame Daphne Sheldrick, helped found the David Sheldrick Wildlife Trust after her husband died in 1977. David was the founder of the Tsavo East National Park, the biggest game park in the country.[1]

Diana and I met Daphne in the late 1980s when she was running the elephant orphanage in the Nairobi National Park. A cheerful, friendly woman of enormous energy and foresight, Daphne achieved world fame by nurturing orphaned elephants and rhinos before releasing them back into the wild.

When we met Daphne we were delighted to be able to touch and bond with the baby animals. We remember Sam, a friendly baby rhino who would trot after people demanding attention.

Although just a youngster he was already rather weighty. But if he bowled you over it would be out of sheer love.

The early years were frustrating for Daphne and she told me of her struggles of finding the right milk formula for the baby elephants. Ordinary milk formulas were tried but did not work. The young elephants wound survive for a while, sometimes for a few months, and then fade away and die. It took Daphne 28 years before she hit on the right formula. So what was the specific ingredient that did the trick? According to Daphne's obituary in the *Guardian* newspaper of 25 April 2018, it was coconut oil![2]

Daphne also initiated a foster scheme for the elephants: you could foster and maintain an elephant for a few dollars a month. Our daughter Imogen was chuffed to have for a few years her very "own" elephant before, she was released back into the wild. Honours from around the world were heaped on Daphne who was born, raised and educated in Kenya. The Kenyan Government awarded her the Moran of the Burning Spear and the Queen made her a Dame in 2006.

The Nairobi National Park is on the doorstep of the city, framed by a backdrop of skyscrapers. On a good day in our time you would see lion, buffalo, giraffe, zebra and maybe a cheetah. On a bad day you might have to settle for zebra, giraffe and gazelle.

The park faces an ever-increasing encroachment of civilisation. Game goes and comes as it pleases, but there is a real threat that the entrance/exit is being pinched from all sides. If that gap is closed, we were told, the park will go from being an open range, to just a large outdoor zoo.

An extract from the Kenyan online publication *Rough Guides.com*[3] gives a graphic account of just how real that threat is. For most of the 20th century, the park enjoyed the second biggest herbivore migrations after that of the Mara-Serengeti. "Thousands of wildebeest and zebra would stream in from the south in July and August for the good grazing.

"Before 1946, when the park was created, only the physical barrier of Nairobi itself diverted what was a general northward migration towards the Aberdare Range and the foothills of Mt Kenya. The erection of fences along the park's northern perimeter closed that migration route, while the steady encroachment of housing, industry, farms and livestock grazing also tightened the wildlife corridor there.

"The wildebeest you see nowadays are mostly sedentary individuals that stay on the park all year, and the migration has been reduced, in most years, to a trickle. Conservationists are, however, determined to keep the southern corridor open, claiming that to fence the park (partly a response to fears about lion and rhino poaching) would effectively suffocate its ecosystem, which depends on free ranging wildlife to be sustainable."

Of course, to watch the annual Mara-Serengeti migration, even if it does not reach the Nairobi Park, is still a breathtaking event. We watched it one year from a high vantage point in the Maasai Mara. Animals streamed in from dozens of separate trails to join one huge trek northward. We were spell-bound.

The Nairobi National Park is still worthy of exploration. It is also close to Wilson Airport that sees much light plane traffic go off to tourist destinations. And it is close to the Carnivore restaurant that specialised, in our time at least, to hungry meat-eaters.

Waiters would come to your table and carve before you such

exotic roasts as gazelle, Kongoni, zebra, giraffe, camel and crocodile. Kongoni, to my palate, is the pick of them all. Zebra tasted like a cross between beef and lamb. Camel was pretty tough. Some say like old boot. And crocodile was a strange cross between fish and chicken, without doing justice to either. It did not appeal.

Chapter 29

THE JADE SEA

In 1993, in an open-sided truck, converted to take about 18 passengers, we set out on one of our greatest adventures. An eight-day return trip to Lake Turkana — the largest desert lake in the world and breeding ground of the Nile crocodile. Lake Turkana is also known as the Jade Sea. It is that exquisite deep green that you see, typically, in Chinese jade ornaments. The colour comes from algae that rise to the surface in warm weather. Fed by the Omo River in Ethiopia, the lake flows north to south for 249 kilometres.

The bulk of its water is in northern Kenya, in the hot arid reaches of the eastern Rift Valley. According to UNESCO, the region is a vital link in the evolutionary history of the human species. The remains of five of five human and pre-human species, including *homo erectus* and early *homo sapiens,* have been discovered in the area. It is a candidate, say experts, as one of the "cradles of mankind".

Our group, which included school teachers and diplomats and their partners and children, set off from Nairobi and followed the Great Rift Valley, which splits much of Africa down the middle, up to where the lake lips Ethiopia at the border.

It was rough camping all the way as our route passed through Naivasha, Nakuru, Nyahururu (Thomson Falls) and lakes Borgoria and Boringo. It was then on to Loruk, Maralal before crossing the Chalbi Desert. At times we passed through dangerous territory, known for bandits. Our helpers warned us to watch for scorpions and snakes when we set up camp.

Our friend and neighbour Kern Roberts chuckled as he recalled how his 12-year-old son, Ryan, bargained with tribesmen in the desert, swapping a tube of toothpaste for a wooden Ethiopian head rest. These objects, which vary in design, are only a few centimetres deep and just wide enough to cradle a head. They are surprisingly comfortable and highly portable because of their light weight. Diana bought several on our way back to Nairobi.

Kern's wife, Susan, remembers a child bursting into tears as we neared Lake Turkana. It was probably the first time she had seen white people, says Susan. By the time we got to Lake Turkana it was boiling hot. The driver and helpers warned us about snakes and scorpions that lived in the immense piles of rocks thrown up during the great eruptions when the Rift Valley was formed. But it was so hot that some of us crawled out of our tents and slept outside. Make your choice: risk being bitten, or being boiled alive.

At the lake, helpers frantically waved their arms and shouted "watch out for the crocodiles" as some in our party raced to the water and its beach-like surrounds.

The children and the young teachers splashed around happily.

Susan was posted on crocodile watch. But there were no crocodiles. "We were beginning to believe our helpers were scare mongers", recalled Susan in a recent email. Then horror shock. Around the next cove were numerous crocodiles basking in the sun.

The bathers had every reason to be shocked. The Turkana region has a population of 14,000 Nile crocodiles (*Crocodylus niloticus*): The greatest number of the species in the world. The lake is also home to the hippopotamus, several snake species and an important passage and stopover for migratory birds.

Packing up from our camp site on the edge of Lake Turkana, near the town of Loiyangalani, we headed back to Nairobi via Marsabit, Archers Post, Embu, Nyeri.

John Murphy and son Ryan make friends with tribesmen on the Lake Turkana trip.

Author John Lawrence strikes camp near Turkana, taking a chance with scorpions and snakes.

We elected not to stay in this hotel.

Our truck finds it rough going on the northern Kenya expedition.

Phil Tilley holding forth

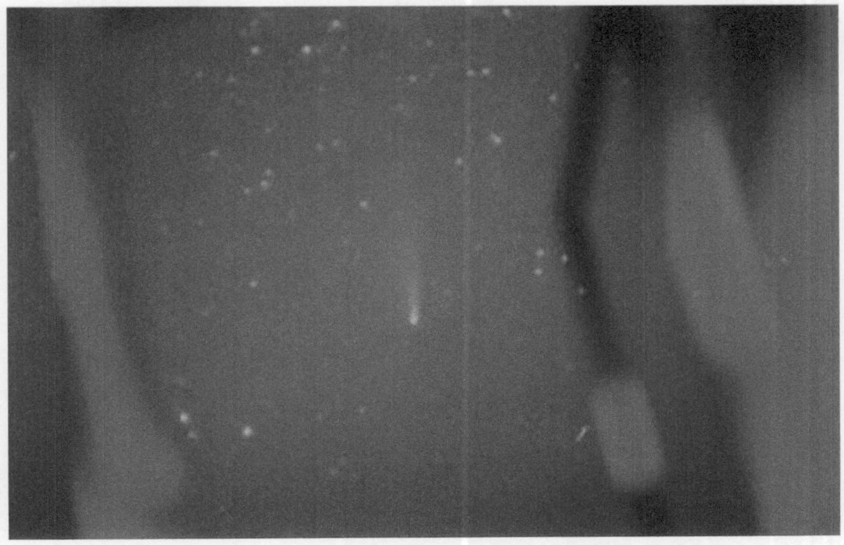

Steve Meacher, a keen photographer, took this shot of Halley's Comet from the window of Twiga Lodge at the game ranch.

We have takeoff. Diana and African guide about to take a balloon flight over the Mara.

Mauritius reunion: Diana and Sadhna Ramlallah get together again after a quarter of a century.

Cat's curiosity. A ranch cheetah (above) peeps in a window and (below) goes for a rooftop stroll.

Sadhna Ramlallah in relaxation mode in Mauritius.

Going my way? Diana was driving past when she came across these two hitch-hiking cheetahs.

Luxury on the Maasai Mara. A well-appointed bedroom in a tented camp site.

Cheers. Carla Viezee (left) and Diana Lawrence toast each other at the game ranch.

Al fresco dining at the Athi River Game Ranch.
From left: David and Carol Hopcraft and Tim Tilley (standing).

Elephants take a drink before crossing a water hole on the Maasai Mara.

A young Duma and ranch dog suss each other out.

An egret stands sentinel.

Gazelle find shelter and sanctuary in the well-camouflaged bush.

Sunset on the Maasai Mara.

Chapter 30

BOOTED OUT

It all happened innocently enough. We had received a letter from our friends, Bronwyn and Peter Jackson, who were managing a tea plantation in Tanzania. They were coming to Nairobi so that Bron, who was largely pregnant, could have her baby in comfort and security. We were overjoyed to see them.

Over a welcoming drink, we put on a Kevin Bloody Wilson tape and laughed ourselves silly to his bawdy but clever, entertaining lyrics. Dinner went well as we re-lived old times and Bron, who had been told she still had another two weeks to run, went to bed happy and relaxed.

However, as so often happens, things began to move quickly and we were awaked about three o'clock in the morning by loud voices and much disturbance coming from the Jackson bedroom.

Bron's baby was on its way.

Speed was of the essence if she was to make the hospital in time. Peter said something like "that was unexpected".

And Bron said:

"It's Kevin Bloody Wilson's fault."

Peter was shocked. "Who's Bloody Kevin Wilson? I thought it was me!" Recounting what happened later, Bron said:

"I laughed so much listening to Kevin Bloody Wilson that my whole body shook. I'm sure that's what got the baby moving." That and a two-day journey from southern Tanzania.

Peter wasted no time, after receiving directions from us, in driving to the Nairobi General Hospital, at one stage making a wrong turn and finding himself and Bron in the driveway of the city morgue. But he made the hospital in time and baby Natalie was born about an hour later without further drama.

Next day, Peter set off to the city to register the birth — and that is when the chain of events, that led up to my deportation started. The Registry of Births, Deaths and Marriages was located in an omnibus of a building called Nyao House, home to many government departments and offices.

Now the basement of the building, it was rumoured, was reserved for torture meted out to dissidents and others by special branch police or the Army's dreaded General Services Unit. One of the methods to induce confessions, again it was rumoured, was to tie and brick or some other heavy weight by string to a man's penis.

Another, allegedly, was to flood a section of the basement so that prisoners had to stand on tiptoes to keep head above water.

Nyao House therefore had a rather sinister reputation. This feeling was compounded when Peter, on his way to register the birth, noticed a putrid smell coming from a vent or manhole near the corner of the building. "It smelt as if a human body had been chopped into pieces, stuffed down there and left to rot," said Peter.

That day I was searching around frantically for a lead to my daily column *The Cutting Edge,* by Watchman. Peter's observation gave the lead I wanted. Wrong move. I had trodden on very sensitive toes. I had started writing *The Cutting Edge* about three years earlier in the belief that the newspaper badly needed a social awareness column that would draw attention to petty sloth, and other vices.

Traffic chaos, festering garbage mounds, bribery of various kinds and petty police corruption became grist to the mill. It was an intuitive, no-names, no-pack drill type of column. It was hugely popular and had the strong support of the *Daily Nation's* top echelon.

Hiding behind my *non de plume,* I had become a sort of community ombudsman. In a nation struggling to come to terms with democracy and widespread corruption, it gave its citizenry a chance to let off steam and vent their many grievances. But I had made fateful mistake in my choice of a lead item, a choice I would not have made in normal circumstances.

For a couple of weeks nothing happened. Then on the afternoon of 11 July, 1994, the phone on my desk rang. It was Reception on the ground floor informing me that three men from the Department of Immigration wanted to see me. I stalled them and reported this alarming news to the Editor, Tom Mshindi, who patched me through to the department's deputy chief, a Mr Adami, who was in no mood to finesse the situation.

"Just get here quick," he barked aggressively down the phone. Within minutes, I was squeezed into a small pick-up truck, accompanied by three minders and driven to the Immigration building. I was locked in a room and told the boss would see me soon. I cannot pinpoint the time, but it must have been about 4pm.

I asked permission to ring my wife.

Permission denied.

I asked permission to ring my office.

Permission denied.

A little later, Diana arrived at the *Daily Nation* on her normal pick-up run and was told I had been detained. Alarmed, she rang the Australian High Commission. High Commission officers, fearing my imminent deportation, made urgent calls to Immigration.

At the same time, Albert Ekirapa, the chairman of the company, was also ringing the department. Official sources deflected the calls with comments like "We will look into this and get back to you", or "ring back in such and such a time and we'll have some news for you". Eventually telephones were simply left off the hook.

Still locked in my room, I made another plea to ring my wife. "Sorry," I was told, "our switchboard has closed for the day.

Lies and prevarications. My chances of release looked bleak. However at last I got a chance to have my say and was ushered into the presence of Mr Adami who was seated behind a large desk in Room 623. Three well-built associates were lounging on a settee. The deputy chief rose, affability written all over his face, and shook my hand.

"Ah, Mr Lawrence, how have you been?" he said with a smile. Hope rose, but I bristled and said: "How would you be if you had been held for several hours and not allowed to ring the office or your wife?"

"Yes, sorry about that, sorry for the delay, but I have to give you this," said Mr Adami, handing me an envelope. I tore it open.

The message was explicit:

"This is to inform you that the Minister of State responsible for Immigration has declared that the entry into or presence within Kenya of yourself is contrary to the national interests. In consequence of this declaration, you are a Prohibited Immigrant for all purposes other than Section 3 of the Immigration Act.

"You are therefore required to depart Kenya immediately, and in this case arrangements have been already made by this Department to leave on board flight No. OA 103 departing Jomo Kenyatta International Airport after midnight today.

"I must warn you that failure to depart as directed, your removal will be enforced under the provisions of the Immigration Act."

The letter, dated 11 July 1994 was signed by F.J.M. Kwinga, Principal Immigration Officer.

I had half expected this outcome, but had hoped it would be confined to a good dressing down and a warning to keep my nose out of domestic Kenyan affairs. Now facing deportation, I drew myself up and in feigned outrage thundered:

"This is an outrage!"

Mr Adami's bland expression didn't change.

"Why am I being deported?" I demanded.

"You mean you don't know?" Mr Adami raised an eyebrow,

but didn't answer the question. After an awkward pause, he said: "Well we must get you to the airport."Then, with a wave at the three men lounging on the couch, added "These men will escort you there."

Back in the room where I had been first detained, the last thing I had expected was summary deportation. Normal procedure, I believed, was to give the deportee reasonable notice — time to put affairs in order, time to pack, time to say goodbyes. Time to withdraw our daughter from Hillcrest Secondary School. Time to arrange flights home for her and Diana. Time to pat the dogs and ensure they would be in good care.

"Look", I said, "I need to go home to say goodbye to my wife and daughter."

"Afraid you can't," said Mr Adami.

"And I will need to pack my clothes. Get some money. Get my medications."

Astoundingly, Mr Adami retorted:

"What do you need money for? We are paying for your flight."

My protests were getting nowhere. Then, abruptly, the deputy Immigration chief relented. "All right, we will take you home briefly and then you will be driven to the airport." Without further ado, I was led to a car. One of the heavies sat next to the driver and the other two climbed into the back. I was Malcolm in the middle.

We had barely gone a kilometre, when I sensed something was wrong. I looked out the window. We were going in the wrong direction. I tapped the driver on the shoulder.

"Hey, this is not the way to my home in Kileleshwa." The driver half-turned, smiled and drove on. To the airport.

While this was going on, frantic moves were being made to have me released and the deportation overturned. Ekirapa, a man with great respect and pull in media, government and business circles, was furiously making phone calls. At the same time the High Commission was ringing all official channels.

Each time they were told inquiries were being made. Or given some spurious excuse. Eventually all Immigration phones were simply left off the hook.

Ekirapa told Diana: "At all cost, he must not get on that plane. Once he's on the aircraft we will never get him off. Tell him to stall all he can."

Again, I asked if I could ring Diana. No, I was told. We'll ring her for you. They didn't say when.

By now it was fast approaching midnight. I was being held in a large spacious room, unattended except for an elderly African seated behind a big ledger through which he was riffling. Briefly I thought of making a run for it. Just as briefly I dismissed the idea.

After an hour or two, I began to hear raised voices through the thin wall of the room. The High Commission, like the cavalry, was making a charge to rescue me. The deputation was led by the Consul, Bruce Curley, and two other officers. I was later told that Immigration or airport officials denied all knowledge of my presence. However, the HC trio persisted and finally it was admitted that I was indeed being held there pending deportation.

More time slipped by and then, at last, a small breakthrough. "Your wife is on the telephone now," said an official. "You may speak to her."

I was patched through. The reassuring voice of Diana came through loud and clear. "Are you okay?" she asked.

"Yes, but bloody angry and frustrated."

"Well", said Diana, always the cool one. "Look on it all as an experience"

Diana was not allowed to see me in person, but she had packed an overnight bag with change of clothes, toiletries, passport and a small amount of cash. I had now been held for close on 10 hours and yearned for a drink and a meal.

"Am I allowed to have a meal," I inquired of my keepers.

"Of course. Certainly you can."

"I assume the Government is paying."

"No, the Government is not paying. You must pay."

I was escorted into the airport dining room where I ordered a Tusker beer and a large rump steak. Eating at leisurely pace, I enjoyed every delicious mouthful, while my three keepers watched on with envy.

My minders were getting edgy and restless. "Are you finished yet?" Asked their spokesman."

"In a minute, but first I must go to the toilet." They followed me and waited. I was enjoying my little stalling game and made them wait a little longer as I made a grand show of washing my hands and combing my hair.

But you can only push things so far and at last I was led onto the Olympic Airways plane. I was barely seated when a smiling Kenyan strode down the aisle with my ticket, my passport and the bag that Diana had packed. The man shook my hand warmly and said:

"Have a nice flight Mr Lawrence."

The plane took off for Johannesburg. It was 4.20 am. I had been detained for more than 12 hours.

Things turned nasty next day, I later learned, when the female Deputy High Commissioner went to the Ministry to protest. A Kenyan immigration officer blew his fuse. "So", he said, "they send a woman here to do a man's job. Is that the way you treat us Africans." There was no disrespect on the part of the High Commission. The High Commissioner was upcountry on official business and his deputy had stepped in to represent him.

Chapter 31

THEN THE STORM

The flight to Johannesburg was uneventful and I arrived to find a High Commission officer waiting to greet me. After the trauma of detention he was a welcome sight. I was booked into a hotel near the airport and the Trade Commissioner, whom I had first met in Nairobi, showed me the delights of hotel life in Jo'burg.

We got uproariously drunk.

I had two nights stay in the hotel at the airline's expense until a connecting Qantas flight from Sydney could arrive. It wasn't long before the telephone calls came flooding in. Ekirapa, disturbed at my sudden and unceremonious departure, rang to ask after my welfare and to assure me that Diana and Imogen were being well looked after.

The chairman of the Parklands Sports Club, where I was on the committee, phoned to assure me that my departure was in no way connected to the club. Evidently there had been rumours that an Immigration officer, a fellow committeeman and drinking buddy, had reported me for remarks made at the bar. The chairman quickly laid rest to the rumours, much to my relief.

Diana rang. So did the Press. Diana herself had had a visit from journalists, amazed to be greeted, not by a distraught spouse, but by a smiling young woman with a glass of bubbles in her hand.

"Shouldn't you be concerned and upset that your husband has been deported," said a reporter.

"Why," replied Diana. "He's okay. He's safe. And besides someone has to drink his grog."

Indeed, it was what I would have wanted. I had built up a fair wine cupboard, but what better way to mark my temporary passing than to have a convivial wake among friends.

Back in Nairobi my sudden removal had created quite a stir. Questions were raised in the Parliament. FORD Kenya urged the Government to withdraw the deportation order and the Australian High Commission, speaking to the Melbourne *Herald-Sun* and Australian Associated Press, said it had been frustrated by Kenya authorities in efforts to receive a reason for the deportation. An HC spokeswoman, Ms Bernadette Siely, said the Australian Government regarded the official charge very seriously and was trying to speak to authorities.[1]

The deportation attracted plenty of headlines.

Expelled journalist not allowed to see wife
(*The Age,* Melbourne)

Aussie journalist deported
(*The Star,* South Africa)

And the one that tickled me pink and gave me bragging rights:

Graft buster deported
(*Herald-Sun*)

The Australian newspaper stories were diligently saved, photo-copied and presented to me on my return to Australia by my daughter Kerrina Lawrence.

In Nairobi, the Kenyan Government's action was front-page news in the *Daily Nation* under the headline: **Govt deports senior Nation editor.** But it was not until 26 July that the Government, pressed for answers, gave some sort of response. In Parliament, the MP for Gem, Dr Oki Ooko Ombaka, put the question to Assistant Minister Moody Awori: Why was John Lawrence, an Australian, deported?

Awori, whose portfolio included the Office of the President, cited State security and contravention of Section 3 of the Immigration Act. Pressed further, Awori refused to elaborate on the grounds that such matters could not be discussed in public.

However, the inference was clear: The order to deport had to come from the top — on the orders of the autocratic Daniel arap Moi.

Dr Ombaka persisted: Why was Mr Lawrence subjected to inhuman treatment, held incommunicado, taken to the airport and refused access to his family? Awori replied that he was not aware of those circumstances.

The MP for Molo, Mr Njenga Mungai, asked the Minister to tell the House what aspect of the law I had contravened. Dr Ombaka chipped in to say that Section 3 of the Immigration Act had 16 items which included prostitution or mental inability.

"Can you tell us which one of these he contravened," he asked.

Awori again refused to disclose. It was a matter of state security, he said.

The above passages (apart from the reference to President Moi) were quoted or adapted from the *Daily Nation* report headlined **Awori: Why 'Nation' editor was deported** and sub-headed **Assistant Minister cites state security.**

A delightful example of the influence that the Watchman wielded came from a priest in the town of Thika who reported having supply problems caused by the KP& Lighting Company. Addressed to "The Mighty Watchman", it said:

> "Dear Sir, I owe you a beer.
>
> "In case you are "saved" it will be tea with an extra helping of imported sugar. I never believed you were so powerful as to catapult five dark-suited and tied gentlemen out of their executive swivel chairs in high-rise Nairobi offices and bundle them expeditiously into my little office only hours after the appearance of your column. Things are elephant: I have advanced from a little unknown country priest into a KP&Lighting V.I.P client. I am guaranteed 24 hours of uninterruptible power supply.
>
> Who else can boast of such luxury in this country of ours? So, just tell me if you prefer a cold beer straight from the kenyapoweredandlightinged (sic) fridge or a steaming hot cup of saved tea?
>
> Salaam
>
> Fr Max Statter

So the African adventure — west coast and east coast — had

finally come to an end. John and Lorna Roberts, my in-laws picked me up from Melbourne International Airport and took me to their farm at Hume Vale near Whittlesea for rest and recuperation. A few weeks later, after a holiday in England and Greece, Diana and Imogen, flew home. We were re-united once more.

Next day, we decided to go out to Melbourne Airport without delay. It was the sort of four-seasons-in-a-day weather for which Melbourne is famous and by the time we got to the freight section it was raining. We filled in the customs declaration and a customs officer accompanied us out to the tarmac where a man on a forklift truck was awaiting us with the crate that held years of accrued possessions.

The customs officer wanted to verify that the contents, particularly items like a Maasai spear, matched our declaration. The rain was getting heavier as the customs officer addressed the forklift man:

"Have you got a jemmy on you so I can open this crate?"

"Waddya think I am mate. A fucking magician?" replied the forklift driver.

Yes. It was good to be back in Australia. And that crate didn't get opened until we got it home.

Epilogue

At the of September 2018, the wheel turned full circle and Diana returned to Kenya to stay, in turn, with Clare Jethwa in her Nairobi home and with Phil and Tim Tilley at the Athi River Game Ranch. It was 24 years since she had seen many of our friends. She was treated liked a prodigal daughter, invited into people's homes, wined and dined at the prestigious Muthaiga Country Club and entertained by Wangethi Mwangi at Parklands Sports Club.

And there were shocks. The comfortable home in leafy Kileleshwa where we had stayed for nearly nine years, was gone. Demolished to make way for a hideous apartment block. Gone were the monkeys that used to swing in from the Arboretum to taunt our dogs and gone were the squirrels and mongooses.

Our lovely garden, with its roses and tropical fruit trees, had vanished under bricks and mortar. It was a garden that had been captured on canvas by an art teacher friend. Next door, the house where our friends Kern and Sue Roberts had stayed, had met a similar fate.

"Nairobi used to be a green city," Diana lamented. "Now, where there were once green hedges, there are concrete fences.

None of the apartment blocks that were going up everywhere seemed to have been landscaped. There was a lack of planning."

The Aboretum, two houses back from our home, however, had received a beneficial makeover. Its excellent collection of exotic trees had been neglected for years and it had become an overgrown jungle. A place where it was unsafe to go at night. Now, it had become a well-managed park.

Physically, the place was going gangbusters. Cranes dominated the landscape, helping to build dozens of five and six-storey slightly old-fashioned apartment blocks. And the Chinese were building and improving roads apace. The traffic was horrendous; the driving aggressive — a game of bluff, said Diana. Yet, astonishingly, everyone still stopped at the traffic lights.

Potholes were as common as ever, but there was artwork at the traffic islands and road junctions. Security was tight and many streets had been converted into gated communities. Strangely, perhaps, Diana noticed no white faces in the city.

A highlight of the return visit was a balloon flight over the Masai Mara. It was something we had planned to do together, but my sudden exit from the country had pre-empted that. Now Diana thrilled at the sight below of the sweeping plains and its animals, but noted that the once verdant grasslands, where game had grazed on the migrations northwards, was a uniform brown.

At the Athi River Game Ranch, Diana dined with the Tilleys and owner Dr David Hopcraft and his American wife, Carol. Phil, she found, was as inventive as ever. The Chinese were in the area and were in urgent need of soil for their roadworks. They approached Phil for help. Sure, said Phil, go ahead. It was a fine quid pro quo: The Chinese got their soil, the Game Ranch got their money and Phil filled in the holes to form beautiful lakes, an environmentally sound move that meshed in nicely with the ranch's eco tourism. Memorial trees were planted.

Diana took the opportunity to meet up with other old friends: Mac Wijenge, a teacher at our daughter's school, Hillcrest, Jackie Guest and her husband, Julius Kinuthia, as well as Gran Calder and Sara Shaw. And also the charismatic and irrepressible Dutch woman, Carla Viezee.

Carla always remains in my memory as the beautiful, scantily young woman who, dagger in mouth and hibiscus flower behind her ear, jumped out of a ribbon-bound box during my 60th birthday celebrations. In May 2019 she made a surprise visit to our home in inner-suburban North Carlton. Minus the box and dagger.

There was sadness, too, when, in March 2019, cancer claimed our good friend Kern Roberts. Shortly before he died, Diana and I, along with John and Evelyn Murphy, were able to talk with him on telephone hook-up. We were holidaying at Merimbula on the New South Wales south coast. Kern and his wife, Susan, had been scheduled to join us from the UK before the illness struck.

Appendix

A CHIMP NAMED STEPHEN

The following story was written by **Don Rooken-Smith**. This is an abridged and lightly edited version which provides valuable insights into the history of the colourful Foster clan and picks up again on Stephen the canny Chimpanzee.

So long as Mary can recall, right up to her early teens, the Fosters of Kaptagat had chimps around the house. In that era in the British colony of Kenya in East Africa, most of us grew up with wild animals — mainly orphans. My own father caught cheetah from horseback, in the mid-30s to sell to the maharajas of India.

One or two ranchers had tried crossing the Cape buffalo with the common cow for increased hybrid vigour and diseased resistance. Raymond Hook had successfully crossed the Grevy zebra with the horse, producing the zebroid. Numerous folk had lion and leopard cubs. And more recently my cousin Daphne Sheldrick was awarded an MBE for her work with orphan elephants.

And so back to Mary and her childhood. This is Stephen's story, told through the eyes of a child growing up in the 1940s and related to me over numerous dinner parties.

But let's start at the beginning. The four Foster brothers, of whom Mary's father Hugh was the youngest, went out to the East Africa country of Uganda in about 1910 to grow coffee and make their fortunes. They fought in various branches of the military in the East African theatre during World War One, and eventually ended up owning and operating cotton ginneries in the Teso district of Uganda. Between times they shot a great number of elephant for their ivory, which helped pay the farm expenses.

Robert, one of the brothers, was killed by a lion in the Belgian Congo (now the Democratic Republic of Congo) in 1919 while he and Hugh were after ivory. Hugh married Zoe in1928, having met her during a rather raucous party at the Imperial Hotel in Kampala. She had walked in from the Congo to see the dentist.

The Fosters bought a farm in the high country of western Kenya and called it Kaptagat Farm.

Zoe was a Yorkshire lass who, in 1919, lost her doctor father and older sister to the Spanish flu epidemic. To get away from it all, she and her mother took a boat trip to Africa. They trekked into the Congo, possibly from the port of Dar es Salaam. On the boat Zoe met, fell in love with and married a handsome hunter called "Congo" Parker. The marriage, like many shipboard romances failed, but produced a daughter, Neville, in 1926.

Some time after leaving Parker, Zoe married Hugh Foster and her mother married Hugh's elder brother Fronny, to become known ever after as Aunt Lil.

My wife's mother Zoe Foster was an extraordinary woman.

Possessed of unlimited drive and willpower, she was instrumental in starting the Kaptagat Preparatory School, the Kaptagat Arms Hotel and the Kaptagat Sports Club. The Foster family made annual pilgrimages to the seaside, travelling 500 miles along dirt roads to Mombasa. [The story of how Zoe discovered, and with husband Hugh, developed Sand Island on Tiwi Beach, is covered in the chapter Island Paradise.]

It was in the mid-1940s that Zoe bought Stephen the chimp from an Asian trader in the streets of Mombasa. He was in a pitiful state of neglect and malnutrition before Zoe nursed him back to health.

I first saw Stephen perform while staying on the farm of a friend when aged about eleven. Zoe, Neville and Stephen were overnight guests and put on a show in the garden. Stephen, was being walked around the garden when he scampered off at high speed. To our astonishment, Neville (then a lovely 20-year-old) picked up a rock and threatened the chimp with it. Stephen slowed down and rather contritely returned to call. We were told that on a previous occasion when Stephen had bolted out of control, Neville picked up a rock and hurled it in frustration. She hit the chimp smack between the eyes and laid him out cold. No permanent damage was done but Stephen never disobeyed again when threatened by a throwing posture.

Stephen lived with the Fosters for perhaps six or seven years. Zoe took him on tour to numerous cinema houses, schools and private shows all over Kenya and Tanganyika (today's Tanzania).

A story that Mary has long dined out occurred on one of the family's annual migrations to the coast. The family broke their journey at the Muthaiga Club in Nairobi, established in 1913 as a settlers' club, and still going strong. It was at the height of colonial decadence. Among the illustrious founding fathers were Lord Delamere, Ewart Grogan, the American Northrup McMillan, Denys Finch-Hatten of Karen Blixen fame, and hosted such characters as the Earl of Errol, Beryl Markham and Edward, Prince of Wales to name just a few.

In the dining room on this morning the Fosters, including Stephen dressed in pants and eating with knife and fork, were having breakfast. Everyone had their noses stuck in newspapers and nothing unusual was noticed for awhile. The secretary (manager) was eventually summoned and, practically speechless, strode through the dining room to observe, among the scruffy children, a chimpanzee eating bacon and eggs.

The normally good, and quietly efficient Englishman, swallowed hard and red-faced declared that monkeys and small children were not allowed in the dining room. To which Zoe retorted: "This is no common monkey. Stephen is much better mannered than any of my children." The club secretary wisely side-stepped the problem. Waiters went back to their assigned tables, breakfast was served and members resumed reading their newspapers. The Fosters evacuated the dining room.

In later years Stephen and another chimp, Sarah, became too large and unruly and delighted in escaping to the nearby Kaptagat school, much to the consternation of teachers. Sadly they were eventually sold and shipped to a zoo in Ceylon (today's Sri Lanka) where one hopes Stephen will be able to put on his pants, drink milk and the odd beer, sweep his room and blow smoke rings for many a year.

Acknowledgements

Many people have given freely of their time, experience and expertise in contributing to this book. First, I wish to thank former foreign correspondent, author, friend and colleague Gerry Loughran in granting permission to quote extensively from his excellent book *Birth of a Nation,* which neatly encompasses both the birth of modern Kenya and the birth of the *Daily Nation,* the premier daily newspaper in East Africa. I have tried to limit my borrowing to that which runs parallel to my own narrative. For example, Loughran refers to my deportation from Kenya and also to some of the problems I faced in training the Nation group's journalists.

I am especially grateful also to the White family, so much a part of the history of Kenya. Geoffrey White, Australian High Commissioner during some of our time there, has supplied valuable background information as well as allowing access to his family memoir. Peter White, a Double Bay solicitor, has filled in gaps relating to the life of his father, Harold, a larger-than-life figure in Kenya, for more than 60 years, until his murder by thugs at the age of 95.

My thanks go to Phil Tilley, a South Australian engineer, who drove into Kenya after an epic round-Africa odyssey and stayed on for 41 years (at last counting). Today, Phil is the manager of Athi River Game Ranch. His life on the ranch and the exotic animals that also live there, has inspired an entertaining chapter.

In Nigeria, I followed two other Australians, Keith Harris and the late John Lahey, to whom this book is in part dedicated, as director of the Nigerian Institute of Journalism. The Australian connection was made possible through the generosity of Ranald Macdonald, former President of the International Press Institute and former managing director and editor-in-chief of *The Age* newspaper in Melbourne. The chairman of the Board of Governors of the Nigerian Institute of Journalism, Alhaji Lateef Jakande, was an inspiration and I received loyal support from my deputy, Gabriel Ogunsekan.

Special thanks also go to Mary Rooken-Smith, last surviving member of the Foster family referred to extensively in this book. I am indebted to her husband, Don Rooken-Smith, who introduced me to a remarkable chimpanzee called Stephen and much valuable family folklore.

Encouragement came from many others, including former colleagues at Deakin University: John Mullen (who provided technical help), Mark Sheehan, Professor Stephen Quinn and especially John Tidey, who gave sound critical advice and wrote the foreword to this book. The documentary maker Andrew Maj gave valuable help in sorting out a couple of picture problems.

Our daughter Imogen Griffiths and husband, James, pressed me to get a move on when I started to flag. Finally, special thanks go to my partner-in-crime, Diana (Dinny) who shared many adventures in both Nigeria and Kenya. As my greatest critic, her sharp memory and eye for detail kept me on my toes throughout the writing of *Ring the Chief Justice*.

End notes

Chapter 4:

1. **Igbo and Ibo**

There is often confusion and argument as to which is correct. According to the New World Encyclopaedia, it is Igbo, sometimes to referred to as Ibo. Most Igbo speakers live in south-eastern Nigeria and constitute about 17 per cent of the population.

2. **Rick Aspinal**

What is lesser known about Rick is that he was married about four times. One of his wives was as Nigerian who first left him, and then returned when he was absent, to clean out and clear off with all the cutlery, clothing and cooking equipment in the house.

Chapter 7:

1. **Lagos water**

Naira Forum (https//www.nairaland.com) gives a good summary of the lagoons, rivers, creeks and other waterways that are a feature of the Lagos landscape.

Chapter 8:

1. **Bush rats**

These giant rats are also called *grass-cutters* in Nigeria and Ghana for their ability to chomp through sugar cane with their strong teeth. They also eat cassava and other cash cops. Grass-cutters are regarded as delicacies and are sometimes farmed or sold in cages. Grown in captivity, they can grow to 6kg or more. You Tube videos even show you ways to cook them.

Chapter 9:

1. **Yoruba clothing**

Nigerians are classy dressers, whether in traditional or western attire. John Lahey remembers seeing a Nigerian coming out of a hovel, dressed like someone straight from a fashion show catwalk. The *fila* mentioned here simply means cap in Yoruba. It is often worn at a rakish angle to the left or right of the head. The *agbada* is flowing formal gown worn over cothes, *gele* is a traditional cloth that women wrap around their heads. Other traditional garments include the *buba,* a long-sleeved blouse, and *sokotos,* trousers with a drawstring to hold them up.

Chapter 10:

1. **Witchcraft**

It is well worth reading the *Encyclopaedia Britannica* article *Juju* by Ibo Change for a comprehensive insight into West African witchcraft. https://www.britannica.com/topic/juju-magic

An Australian woman during our stay, surname *Christmas,* was an acknowledged expert on juju magic. Unfortunately, I have not been able to make contact in the intervening years.

Chapter 11:

1. **The Ransome-Kutis**

More on this famous Nigerian family can be found under the December 2011 *Guardian* online piece *Great dynasties: the Ransome-Kutis.*

Chapter 12:

1. **Language**

Failure to recognise collective nouns was even greater in Nigeria than in Kenya. Some examples collected from the daily newspapers: the deads, beyond repairs, equipments, machineries, luggages, baggages, funs, rubbles, dirts, traffics, shoppings, fightings, in the courses of his duties, bushy hairs.

2. **Jakande jailed**

I was shocked when I learned of Alhaji Lateef Jakande's conviction and jailing for treason. Jakande was considered by many as one of the architects of modern Nigeria. The accusation that he was plotting to overthrow the Government was laughable as Jakande, in his own words, had no arms and no troops. He was jailed for seven years, but pardoned when democracy was restored in 1999.

Chapter 16:

1. **Kilimanjaro**

There are many versions of how Tanganyika (Tanzania) gained possession of Mt Kilimanjaro. The most popular and long-running theory was that Queen.

Victoria gifted the mountain to her grandson, Kaiser Wilhelm 11, on his birthday. Today, this is generally regarded as a myth.

Chapter 17:

1. **Elephant deaths**

The *Guardian* report had this to say: Around 20,000 African elephants were killed last year (2015) for their tusks, more than were born. Chinese wealth is financing a hunger for ivory that threatens to bring to an end wild elephants within our lifetime."

Chapter19:

1. **Forest destruction**

There is a flip side to this. The charcoal sellers, and maybe the tree-fellers, often have an onerous choice: Sell or starve.

Chapter 24:

1. **The Lunatic Express**

Nearly 2,500 indentured Indians and an unknown number Africans died from accidents, tribal raids and marauding lions during construction of the railway between 1890 and 1901.

Index

www.ingramcontent.com/pod-product-compliance
Ingram Content Group UK Ltd.
Pitfield, Milton Keynes, MK11 3LW, UK
UKHW041637190726
13854UKWH00006B/2549

9 781925 984811